Legends of Warfare
NAVAL

US Coast Guard Cutter 37
Formerly Known as USCGC *Taney*

DAVID DOYLE

Schiffer
Military History
4880 Lower Valley Road
Atglen, PA 19310

Other Schiffer books by the author

USS Indianapolis (CA-35): From Presidential Cruiser, to Delivery of the Atomic Bombs, to Tragic Sinking in WWII,
978-0-7643-6262-0

USS North Carolina (BB-55): From WWII Combat to Museum Ship,
978-0-7643-5563-9

USS Hornet (CV-8): From the Doolittle Raid and Midway to Santa Cruz,
978-0-7643-5862-3

Copyright © 2025 by David Doyle

Library of Congress Control Number: 2025930097

All rights reserved. No part of this work may be reproduced or used in any form or by any means—graphic, electronic, or mechanical, including photocopying or information storage and retrieval systems—without written permission from the publisher.

The scanning, uploading, and distribution of this book or any part thereof via the Internet or any other means without the permission of the publisher is illegal and punishable by law. Please purchase only authorized editions and do not participate in or encourage the electronic piracy of copyrighted materials.

"Schiffer Military History" and "pen and inkwell" are trademarks of Schiffer Publishing, Ltd.

Designed by Alexa Harris
Type set in Impact/Universe Lt Sd/Minion Pro

ISBN: 978-0-7643-6966-7
Printed in India
10 9 8 7 6 5 4 3 2 1

Published by Schiffer Publishing, Ltd.
4880 Lower Valley Road
Atglen, PA 19310
Phone: (610) 593-1777; Fax: (610) 593-2002
Email: Info@schifferbooks.com
Web: www.schifferbooks.com

For our complete selection of fine books on this and related subjects, please visit our website at www.schifferbooks.com. You may also write for a free catalog.

Schiffer Publishing's titles are available at special discounts for bulk purchases for sales promotions or premiums. Special editions, including personalized covers, corporate imprints, and excerpts, can be created in large quantities for special needs. For more information, contact the publisher.

We are always looking for people to write books on new and related subjects. If you have an idea for a book, please contact us at proposals@schifferbooks.com.

Acknowledgments

This book would not have been possible without the generous help of Bob Ketenheim, Rich Kolasa, Tom Kailbourn, Dana Bell, Scott Taylor, A. D. Baker III, Sean Hert, and Tracy White—and especially my wonderful wife, Denise, who has given me constant support and encouragement throughout my work on this and dozens of other books.

Any photos not otherwise credited are from the author's collection.

Contents

INTRODUCTION		004
CHAPTER 1	Construction	006
CHAPTER 2	Pre–World War II Service	018
CHAPTER 3	*Taney* in World War II	025
CHAPTER 4	Post–World War II Service	069
CHAPTER 5	Museum Ship	092

Introduction

The Coast Guard Act of January 28, 1915, combined the US Revenue Cutter Service, which had been created in 1790, and the United States Life-Saving Service to form the United States Coast Guard. But for a brief (1967–2003) period of time under the jurisdiction of the Department of Transportation, and today operating under the Department of Homeland Security, from its inception the United States Coast Guard operated under the jurisdiction of the Department of the Treasury. The exception to this was during wartime. The 1915 act states, "The Coast Guard . . . shall operate under the Treasury Department in time of peace and as a part of the Navy, subject to the orders of the Secretary of the Navy, in time of war or when the President shall so direct."

Throughout its existence, the Coast Guard has operated vessels in a variety of sizes. The service's ships with permanent crews and lengths in excess of 65 feet are referred to as cutters. The largest and most capable of the service's ships of the pre–World War II era were the "Cruising Cutters, First Class."

The passage of the Eighteenth Amendment to the US Constitution on January 16, 1919, greatly increased the workload of the Coast Guard. This amendment, commonly known as Prohibition, gave rise to a vast increase in smuggling, with the Coast Guard making efforts to halt the rumrunners—as well as opium smugglers—which ultimately proved easier to do at sea than near shore.

By 1933, the nation was in the grips of the Depression, and although there were many indications that the Twenty-First Amendment (which would repeal the Eighteenth Amendment) would pass, the Coast Guard was badly in need of new vessels, especially large vessels.

The National Industrial Recovery Act of June 1933 included provisions to fund "Construction Projects Recommended for Emergency Public Works." On August 8, 1933, RAdm. H. G. Hamlet, commandant of the Coast Guard, wrote to Secretary of the Treasury William H. Woodin, via Assistant Secretary Stephen B. Gibbons, who was directly over the Coast Guard, describing the need for funding for several Coast Guard projects, including replacements for six obsolete cruising cutters, then between twenty-four and thirty-six years old, as well as three new identical cutters to serve stations then of increasing importance in Unalaska, Alaska, and San Pedro, California, and the Canal Zone.

Attached to the letter was a memorandum that had been sent to the Federal Employment Stabilization Board on May 25, which outlined the essential parameters for the replacement vessels, as follows:

> With due regard to the development of shipbuilding design and the needs of the service, these replacement vessels should be cutters of about 2,000 tons displacement and 20 knots speed. Experience has demonstrated the desirability of increased speed for cruising cutters, and a speed of 20 knots is in agreement with the limitation of armament treaty wherein certain technical characteristics which cruising cutters can possess are outlined. It is proposed to make these new cutters of simple but sturdy design with the facilities and equipment aboard which development of Coast Guard duties demonstrates will be necessary for future operations. For instance, it is proposed to provide salvage gear for airplanes as well as for vessels[,] and, if practicable, an airplane will be carried aboard for searching and observation purposes under favorable conditions. It is increasingly evident that certain cutters will require equipment of novel design to undertake rescue and assistance work for aircraft flying the ocean traffic lanes. It is anticipated the availability of an airplane with each of these new cruising cutters may reduce somewhat the cruising of the vessel itself so that minor economies may result. Primarily, however, the increase in size of the proposed cutters, of from 250 feet long, for the last ten cutters built, to about 300 feet long, is for the purpose of obtaining an increase in speed to 20 knots.

The memorandum continued to make the case for large, capable ships in the subsequent paragraphs:

The two essential needs of the Coast Guard in vessels designed for saving life and offshore assistance and patrol work are seaworthiness and speed.

Increasing demands upon the resources of the service within recent years, due largely to improved methods of communication, resulting from the development of radio, have emphasized these needs. A few minutes gained in arriving at the scene of a disaster may measure the difference between success and failure in an effort to save life.

The radius of operations of the vessels of the service is constantly increasing. It is not unusual to receive calls for assistance from large vessels several hundred miles at sea, and occasionally from vessels as far as 1,000 miles offshore. This type of work calls for larger vessels, for the responding ship must be able to maintain a sustained speed even under adverse weather conditions, and after assuring the safety of the personnel may have to tow the ship several hundred miles to port through winter gales. For this type of work[,] seaworthiness is the prime essential.

Due to the great increase in air traffic the problem of assistance to aircraft is one of great importance. A plane forced down at sea is comparatively helpless, and unless it is reached promptly[,] loss of life may result. In rescue work involving this type of craft[,] speed is the governing requirement, but stability and space for salvaged material are also important.

Both seaworthiness and speed are intimately connected with size and displacement. While the utmost attainable speed and the greatest possible seaworthiness are the characteristics desired in the operation of the Coast Guard, practical considerations limit the attainment of each of these qualities. The limitations are set by the technical aspects of the problem, both from a shipbuilding and an operations viewpoint. A further restriction is the London Naval Treaty of 1930[,] which provides that combatant vessels greater than 2,000 tons [of] standard displacement[,] or of a speed greater than 20 knots, are to be classed as effective tonnage subject to the limitations imposed by the terms of the treaty. Were these limitations not set[,] it might be said that the general increase in speed of passenger vessels to a figure above 20 knots, and the increase in the speed of cargo vessels to a figure around 15 knots[,] would call for a speed on the part of vessels built for assistance work greater than the 20 knots allowed under the terms of the treaty.

The design of a 20[-]knot vessel of less than 2,000 tons standard displacement involves a number of technical problems to the ship designer that can only be solved by the installation of much[-]higher powers, with a consequent increase in operating costs, or a fining of the hull design at the expense of seaworthiness and durability.

It may be stated that a careful study of the entire problem, both from a design and an operating standpoint, has indicated the desirability and reasonableness of planning ships of 2,000 tons standard displacement and 20 knots sustained speed for the class of ships destined for offshore cruising duty. The need for larger cutters to carry an airplane is daily becoming more apparent. In its Alaskan work and patrol of the Bering Sea, in the patrol of the North Atlantic for protection of shipping against icebergs, [and] in searching for derelicts or floating craft, including disabled airplanes, the value of a plane as part of the equipment of a cutter, both from the standpoint of efficiency and economy[,] is readily apparent.

The Coast Guard memorandum continued to emphasize the importance of the new cutters being capable of handling aircraft in the portion of the memorandum dealing with the overall aircraft needs of the service, saying,

Priority No. 5. Seaplanes (9) and equipment for nine 300-foot cruising cutters.

While this item is carried last in the priorities assigned to aircraft in the program submitted, it is believed that the importance of the aircraft equipment feature of the proposed replacement program for cruising cutters warrants especial consideration of this item.

These seaplanes are essential equipment for the type of cruising cutter proposed[,] and in view of the limited number of planes available to the Coast Guard in its general work, it is believed that the feature of mobility provided by the assignment of planes to the type of ship proposed warrants a higher degree of consideration than the priority given would otherwise indicate.

So sure was the Coast Guard of the capabilities of the proposed new cutters that the memorandum stated, "The cruising cutters contemplated by the Coast Guard will be used for the most important work of the service during at least the next twenty years." This would prove an understatement, since all these ships, with the exception of *Hamilton*, which was torpedoed and sunk in January 1942, would serve at least forty-three years, with the average service life of forty-eight years.

CHAPTER 1
Construction

The US Coast Guard Treasury-class (sometimes called Secretary class) cutter that would be formally named USCGC *Roger B. Taney* and, later, *Taney* was initially referred to as Cutter No. 68. These 327-foot cutters were the largest Coast Guard ships until the arrival of the Hamilton class of high-endurance cutters in 1967. Assembly of *Taney* begins as workers position a section of her keel on wooden blocks in Drydock 3 at the Navy Yard, Philadelphia, Pennsylvania, on April 3, 1935. *Ketenheim collection*

On September 21, 1933, Harold L. Ickes, Public Works Administration administrator, announced Federal Project 23A, providing $10,160,000 for the construction of six large cutters capable of carrying aircraft at $1,510,000 each, as well as two $550,000 165-foot cutters. In addition, $1,895,000 was provided to purchase thirty-one seaplanes. *The Baltimore Sun* at the time stated, "Three of the larger cutters will replace the *Snohomish*, the *Seneca* and the *Yamacraw*, each of which is more than 24 years old. The other three are to operate from Coast Guard Stations at Unalaska, Alaska, San Pedro, California, and the Canal Zone." By January 1934 funding for a seventh large cutter had been provided.

Below the waterline and in terms of machinery, the new cutters would have much in common with the Navy's Erie-class gunboats, which also were being built with Public Works Administration funds, construction of these two vessels having been authorized in June 1933.

One of the ships, US Coast Guard Cutter 71, would be built in the Charleston Navy Yard. Two, US Coast Guard Cutters 69 and 70, were to be built in Drydock 2 at the New York Navy Yard.

The remaining four, US Coast Guard Cutters 65, 66, 67, and 68 were built simultaneously in Drydock 3 at the Philadelphia Navy Yard, the contract for their construction having been awarded on March 17, 1934. The decision was made to construct the cutters in the drydock rather than on traditional building ways because it was intended to lay down US Navy cruisers on the ways.

On Friday, April 6, 1934, it was announced that the seven new cutters would be named for seven early secretaries of the treasury. Given the connection between the Coast Guard and the Treasury Department when the construction of a new group of Cruising Cutters, First Class was being contemplated, it is not surprising that the decision was made that these ships would bear the names of past secretaries of the treasury, and the group of ships as a whole would be referred to as Treasury-class cutters.

More of the keel of Cutter No. 68 is viewed from the aft port quarter on April 3, 1935. Under the keel, from the center of the photo to the left, the bottom shell plate has been installed. The shell was the outer skin of the hull. Three other cutters of the Treasury class were also constructed in the same drydock as work proceeded on Cutter No. 68; all would be launched on the same date. *Ketenheim collection*

The formal keel-laying ceremony for Cutter No. 68 was conducted on May 1, 1935, almost a month after the actual laying of the keel. In this ceremony, which normally marked the official start of construction of a ship, Capt. Julius A. Furer, manager of the Industrial Department of the Philadelphia Navy Yard, is ready to drive the "first" rivet with a big riveting machine; he is in the background to the right of center, with his hand on the operating lever of the machine.

The progress of construction of Cutter No. 68 is documented in this June 27, 1935, photograph, taken above the aft starboard quarter of the hull. In the foreground, some of the plates of the double bottom—the inner layer of the hull—have been installed to the sides of the keel. In the background, a watertight lateral bulkhead is in place. Scaffolding is to the sides of the hull. *Ketenheim collection*

Coast Guard Cutter No. 68, which would be given the name *Roger B. Taney*, is in Drydock 3 to the right, next to sister ship *Samuel D. Ingham*, Cutter No. 66, shortly before their launching day, June 3, 1936. The christening stands, platforms from which the cutters' sponsors would dash bottles of champagne against the bows, are visible to the fronts of the bows. *Ketenheim collection*

All four Treasury-class cutters in Drydock 3 at the Philadelphia Navy Yard have been prepared for their christening day, June 3, 1936. They are dressed with flags and pennants fore and aft, and display jacks and bunting on their bows. *Roger B. Taney* is in the right background, with *Samuel D. Ingham* to her side. In the foreground are *George W. Campbell* (*right*) and *William J. Duane* (*left*). Ketenheim collection

The names selected for the cutters were as follows:

Coast Guard Cutter 65: *George W. Campbell*
Coast Guard Cutter 66: *Samuel D. Ingham*
Coast Guard Cutter 67: *William J. Duane*
Coast Guard Cutter 68: *Roger B. Taney*
Coast Guard Cutter 69: *Alexander Hamilton*
Coast Guard Cutter 70: *John C. Spencer*
Coast Guard Cutter 71: *George M. Bibb*

As previously mentioned, the construction of these ships was funded by the Public Works Administration, a New Deal agency (not to be confused with the Works Progress Administration) that sought to improve the national economy by creating jobs for skilled workers through contracts awarded either to private firms or government facilities. Indeed, not only did the construction of the cutters provide the service with the ships that they needed, but it also achieved the goal of the Public Works Administration, with the *Portsmouth Star* reporting on May 2, 1935: "Speaking of present and future activities of the Philadelphia Navy Yard, Capt. J. A. Furer, the yard manager there, states that with the laying of the keels of four new coast guard [*sic*] cutters the Philadelphia Navy Yard is embarking on 'projects employing the greatest army of civilian workers ever engaged in construction at that naval station.' Men will be taken on as the work progresses, and we expect the employment peak to be reached late this fall, when the number of workers will far exceed the former high during the rush years of the World War."

Workers at the Philadelphia Navy Yard began assembling the keel of *Taney* on blocks at the bottom of Drydock 3 on April 3, 1935, almost a full month before the formal keel-laying ceremony on May 1.

Rising from that keel would be a 327-foot-long cutter powered by two Westinghouse double-reduction-geared turbines developing 6,200 horsepower. The length of the ship and her sisters gave rise to the shortened reference to the Treasury-class ships as the "327s." She had a 41-foot beam and would draw 12.5 feet of water at 2,482 tons of displacement when finished.

Work on *Taney* and her sisters progressed at a steady pace, in part driven by total tonnage limits imposed by the London Naval Treaty of 1930, under which the Coast Guard was going to be required to scrap by December 31, 1936, several former Navy destroyers that were among the largest vessels in Coast Guard service.

On June 3, 1936, Philadelphia resident Corinne Taney, the great-grandniece of Secretary Taney and the ship's sponsor, smashed a bottle of champagne on the bow of the ship, christening the

The honor of christening a ship went to a person, usually a woman, designated the sponsor. For the cutter *Roger B. Taney*, the sponsor was Miss Corinne F. Taney, the great-grandniece of Roger B. Taney. In this formal portrait at the christening, she is holding the ceremonial bottle of champagne and a bouquet of roses. *Ketenheim collection*

Corinne F. Taney and a US Coast Guard officer stand on the christening platform on June 3, 1936. Affixed to the rails on the sides of the forecastle are placards that read "U.S.C.G. CUTTER ROGER B. TANEY." Protruding from the sides of the bow are the hawsepipes, which will hold the anchors (not yet installed) when raised.

vessel the *Roger B. Taney*. During the same ceremony, Miss Lucia Brown christened the *George W. Campbell*, Miss May Duane christened the *William J. Duane*, and Mrs. Katherine Brush christened the *Samuel D Ingham*.

Recalling the ceremony years later in an interview with *Navy Times*, the by then Corinne Taney Marks said,

There were four ships christened that day—the *Campbell*, *Duane*, *Ingham*, and the *Taney*. They were christened in alphabetical order. I was told that I should say a few words. I wrote a few words and pined them inside my purse.

It was 3 degrees in Philadelphia on the day of the ceremony, and the woman who christened *Ingham* was dressed in a black dress and a black hat, much more sophisticated than I. I was wearing a turquoise dress with red buttons and a red hat. When

Miss Taney smashes the ceremonial bottle of champagne against the bow of the *Roger B. Taney*, to christen the ship. *Ketenheim collection*

the other woman got up to speak, she said, "I am as honored as I am gratified. Thank you." Well, I was thrown for a loss.

When it was *Taney*'s turn to be christened, I got up and said, "Commandant and ladies and gentlemen," [but] then I couldn't remember anything else. I paused and everyone laughed. Then I remembered my words. Her brothers later told her she said, "Dammit. I knew I would forget what I wanted to say."

Among the dignitaries providing over the christening of the four cutters were Adm. H. G. Hamlet, commandant of the Coast Guard, and Adm. W. C. Watts, commandant of the Philadelphia Navy Yard and commander of the Fourth Naval District.

Following their "launching"—which, because they were built in a drydock, had amounted to merely flooding the drydock, a process that preceded their christenings—*Taney* and her sisters were fitted out.

During the fitting-out period, the myriads of smaller items needed to make the ship both functional and livable were installed: lights, hammocks, numerous small instruments, etc. After the end of the fitting-out period, the ship was commissioned, at which time she became a unit of the US Coast Guard, even while the fitting out was ongoing. This occurred at 1000 on October 24, 1936. Commander (later rear admiral) Eugene Coffin was in command of the *Roger B. Taney*.

The December 1936 US Naval Institute *Proceedings* reported the ship assignments as announced on October 21:

> Moving part of its best equipment into a war against narcotic smuggling from the Orient, the (Coast Guard) Headquarters reshuffled originally announced vessel assignments to station three crack new cutters in the Pacific.
>
> Announcing the move, the Treasury said it was designed to give "increased cooperation" by the Coast Guard to a current drive against this smuggling by all Treasury law enforcement agencies.
>
> The three cutters, *Samuel D. Ingham*, *William J. Duane*, and *Roger B. Taney*, part of the group of seven new 327-foot, 20-knot vessels, will be assigned to Port Angeles, Washington, San Francisco, and Honolulu, respectively. Two originally had been assigned to Boston and one to Honolulu with a cutter going to the latter station some time next spring. Under the reassignment, the *Roger B. Taney*, now nearing completion at the Philadelphia Navy Yard, will be sped to Honolulu possibly this month.

This series of interior photos of the *Roger B. Taney* was taken around the time of the ship's launching in mid-1936. Located on the 02 level (two levels above the main deck) was the pilothouse, alternatively referred to as the wheelhouse or the navigating bridge, with the steering wheel (or helm), operated by the helmsman, to the left. To the left of the wheel is the engine-order telegraph, a mechanical device used to send orders on the speed and direction of the engine. To the front of the wheel are a magnetic compass and a gyrocompass repeater. The two handwheels below the ceiling were for controlling searchlights on the roof of the pilothouse. *Ketenheim collection*

The aft part of the pilothouse is viewed from the starboard side of the steering wheel. To the left is a ladder down to the 01 level. Mounted on the trunk to the right of center are three sound-powered telephone handsets. *Ketenheim collection*

Located in the superstructure on the 01 level (one level above the main deck), the captain's cabin was furnished with upholstered chairs and sofa, a rolltop desk, and a round table. The porthole lenses are raised and secured, for ventilation; curtains are to the sides of each porthole. Above the door to the right, on the aft bulkhead of the cabin, is a small clock. *Ketenheim collection*

Also, on the rear bulkhead of the captain's cabin (*left*) are a wooden buffet with silver service on top, above which is a window to the pantry, located to the rear of the captain's cabin. The door to the left of center led to the captain's stateroom. *Ketenheim collection*

In the aft part of the superstructure on the 01 level was the radio room. The view is from the rear of the compartment, facing forward. Here, radiomen monitored receivers for official communications and distress calls and sent out messages by transmitters. In the foreground are two stations for operators, with radio consoles, desks, typewriters (for typing messages received), and swiveling chairs. *Ketenheim collection*

The warrant officer's stateroom was a compact compartment, with a berth, desk, and chair. Above the berth are a fan and a porthole. Behind the door to the right is a lavatory. *Ketenheim collection*

The commissioned officers of *Taney* took their meals in the wardroom, belowdecks. The space also was used for briefings and meetings. Meals for the commissioned officers were prepared in a pantry adjacent to the wardroom. *Ketenheim collection*

Chief petty officers were fed in this space, the original CPO mess, which later was moved to another area. The mess also was available for CPOs to relax in when off duty. *Ketenheim collection*

CONSTRUCTION 13

A crew's berthing compartment contains bunks, with those to the right triced up for ease of passage through the area. In the right background are crew lockers, where they stowed clothing and personal effects. *Ketenheim collection*

In the galley, meals were prepared for some one hundred crewmen. In the foreground are a wooden chopping block and a preparation table, with an electric mixer to the rear of the table. Pots and pans are stowed below the table. To the left is a cooking kettle. *Ketenheim collection*

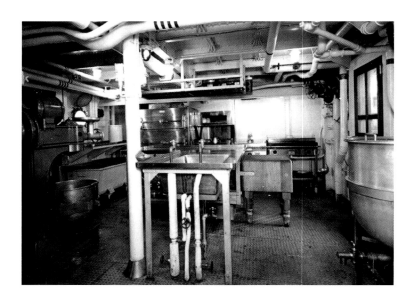

Another view of the galley shows a sink in the center foreground, a chopping block to the rear of the sink, a cooking oven in the left background, and a cooking kettle to the right. *Ketenheim collection*

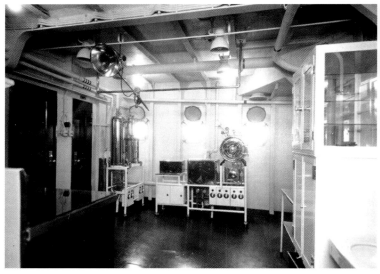

Taney's sick bay, also referred to as the hospital, was located in the superstructure on the main deck and included facilities for medical care, ranging from minor injuries to those requiring surgery. It also included a compartment for quarantining ill crewmen if necessary. In this view, to the left is the operating table, while sterilizers are in the center background. To the right is a glass cabinet for medical equipment, and to the far right is a lavatory. *Ketenheim collection*

In the depths of the center of the hull of *Taney* was the boiler room, holding two Babcock & Wilcox oil-fired, superheating boilers, which generated steam for propelling the two Westinghouse double-geared turbines. To the left is the control panel, containing numerous gauges for monitoring the boilers. *Ketenheim collection*

Two long, narrow compartments known as shaft alleys housed the two propeller shafts as they proceeded from the reduction gears to the propellers. Depicted here is the port shaft alley. Part of the shaft is visible to the lower left; to the right, below the shaft, is a catwalk. *Ketenheim collection*

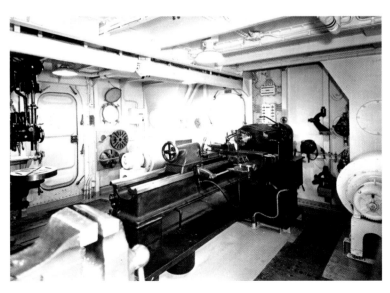

A machine shop is an essential element of any ship, to facilitate the repair of most any system or component of the ship. Dominating this image of *Taney*'s machine shop is a 14-inch lathe for machining metal. In the left foreground is a vise, to the rear of which is a drill press. Also housed in this shop were welding equipment, grinders, and saws. *Ketenheim collection*

CONSTRUCTION 15

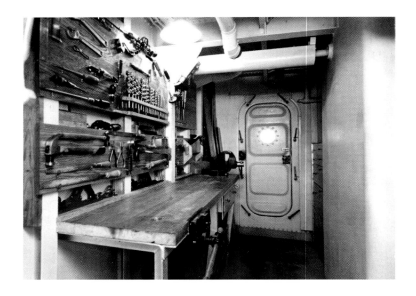

The ship's carpenter was responsible for maintenance and repairs of the wooden parts of the ship, including decks, furniture, and boats. He also was in charge of shoring up damage to the hull with timbers in the event of damage or an attack. The carpenter's shop was very compact, with a workbench, vises, and storage for hand tools. Stored below the bench is a miter box and saw. *Ketenheim collection*

In *Taney*'s armory were stored small arms for use in the cutter's policing activities, such as interdicting drug and arms smugglers and inspecting suspect vessels. To the left is a rack with two shotguns at the top, below which are two Lewis machine guns, one Colt Monitor submachine gun with a recoil compensator on the muzzle, and a Thompson submachine gun. Stored vertically behind these weapons are two Browning M2 .50-caliber machine guns, with water-cooling jackets installed over the barrels. To the right is a rack in which are stored dozens of M1903 Springfield rifles. *Ketenheim collection*

On the 02 level of *Taney*'s superstructure, to the front of the pilothouse, were two naval 6-pounder guns, on pedestal mounts. These pieces were used for firing salutes. *Ketenheim collection*

One of *Taney*'s two Browning M2 .50-caliber machine guns is installed on a pedestal mount. The gun is equipped with a water-cooling sleeve for the barrel, and a white ammunition chest is on the side of the receiver. The frame made of bent pipes is a depression rail, intended to physically prevent the gun from being aimed at any structures on the ship. The rod attached to the cooling jacket was part of this arrangement. *Ketenheim collection*

On the quarterdeck of *Taney* were two fittings used in towing or ungrounding ships in emergency situations. In the foreground, in a view facing to port and aft, is a towing capstan, manufactured by the Silent Hoist and Crane Company, Brooklyn, New York. On the far side of the capstan is a towing bitt, to which a heavy-duty towing line would be fastened. *Ketenheim collection*

CHAPTER 2
Pre–World War II Service

The cutter *Taney* was formally inducted into the service of the US Coast Guard on October 24, 1936. The ship is seen during a shakedown cruise shortly after the commissioning. An awning has been erected over the quarterdeck and fantail. *Ketenheim collection*

Roger B. Taney was not yet fully ready for service when, during a trial run off Cape May on December 2, 1936, she answered a distress call from the Socony tanker *Brilliant*, which had become disabled due to a broken piston. Such would be the service of *Taney* for decades to come, her crew always at the ready to deal with whatever circumstances lay ahead. *Brilliant*'s crew made repairs and continued their journey, and *Taney* and her crew continued sea trials.

On December 19, 1936, *Roger B. Taney* left a snowy Philadelphia on her last, and longest, trial run, steaming at an average of 18 knots to the US West Coast. En route to San Diego, she passed through the Panama Canal December 27–29. After spending one day in San Diego, she steamed to San Pedro, tying up there for two days before moving on to San Francisco to take on 50 tons of registered and special-delivery mail and twenty-one passengers (eleven wives and ten children of her officers) before steaming for Hawaii on January 12, where she would serve as the flagship of the Coast Guard in the Hawaiian Territory.

Arriving at Pier 12 in Honolulu on Monday, January 18, having steamed 7,600 miles from Philadelphia, *Roger B. Taney* relieved her sister ship *William J. Duane*, which had been on temporary duty in Hawaii. *Duane* would return to the West Coast.

On March 13, 1937, *Roger B. Taney*, in port at Honolulu, hurriedly recalled her crew and steamed from port to aid the 5,000-ton British motor ship *Silver Larch*, which had sent a distress signal for any available ship to pick up her four passengers as her crew fought a fire that was sweeping through one of her cargo holds. Ultimately, the passengers were taken off by USS *Louisville*, which arrived earlier, and *Taney* escorted the *Silver Larch* to port, where the fire was extinguished and repairs effected.

On May 28, *Roger B. Taney* made another hurried dash from Honolulu, steaming at top speed to rendezvous with the yacht *Viking*, owned by financier George Fisher Baker Jr., then the third-wealthiest American, behind only Henry Ford and John D. Rockefeller. Aboard the yacht, Baker had fallen gravely ill, believed to be suffering from peritonitis. *Taney* reached the *Viking* shortly after 3:00 a.m., fourteen and a half hours after leaving port. Ultimately, despite these efforts, Baker died aboard his yacht at Pier 7 in Honolulu on May 30.

The next month, *Roger B. Taney* had scheduled drydocking beginning on June 14. Two days later, many of her crew transferred temporarily to the cutter *Itasca*, which was lending navigational support for Amelia Earhart's ill-fated flight to Howland Island. While some texts state that *Taney* participated in the subsequent search for Earhart, the big cutter was in fact in drydock at the time and unable to join in the fruitless search.

However, in March 1938 the men of the *Roger B. Taney* did make a headline story when the ship was central in an international incident. As the *Oakland Tribune* reported,

> In a move made dramatic by its secrecy, the United States today was in possession of British-claimed Canton and Enderbury Islands in the South Pacific and had precipitated what may be an international incident.
>
> When the White House announced its intention to claim the islands, valuable as airplane bases on the United States–New Zealand route, after colonization parties already had been landed from the Coast Guard cutter *Roger B. Taney*, British officialdom was aroused.
>
> In the House of Commons, Parliament members said they would demand that Prime Minister Neville Chamberlain explain what the British Government is doing to "preserve British rights."

Elaborating on the secret operation, the *Tribune* reported,

> The cutter *Taney* received coded orders direct from Washington and a few days later, on February 27, left Honolulu for the South Pacific islands with colonists and colonizing equipment aboard.

> Last Sunday—South Pacific time or Saturday in the United States, five Hawaiians, all United States citizens, were landed from the *Taney* on Canton[,] and on Sunday (United States time) four were placed on Enderbury. While the colonists were preparing their homes for the next six months at least, sailors from the Coast Guard cutter were planting the American flag on both islands.
>
> The *Taney* was under instructions to report directly to Washington and not through the San Francisco headquarters of the Coast Guard as is usual for Coast Guard vessels cruising in the Pacific.

One of the benefits of the American "occupation" of the Canton and Enderbury Islands was an agreement to allow Pan American Airways to operate both seaplane and landplane bases from Canton. This allowed the company to abandon its cramped and dangerous facility at Pago Pago.

Some of these activities were reported by William Norwood in the *Honolulu Star-Bulletin*, which on July 8, 1939, published a recap of Norwood's experiences aboard *Roger B. Taney*:

> The *Taney* departed from Honolulu at 5 p.m. Saturday with relief personnel and supplies for equatorial islands and with equipment and personnel for Pan American Airway's new base at Canton.

Following her shakedown period, *Taney* departed from the East Coast for her first assigned station, Honolulu, Oahu, Hawaii Territory. The cutter is seen after her January 18, 1937, arrival at that base. A large awning is rigged above the fantail and the quarterdeck, and a rolled-up awning is suspended above the forward deck. Form-fitting covers are over the cutter's guns.

For several years after her posting in Honolulu, *Taney* made periodic cruises to the US-held Line Islands, on or near the equator some 1,500 miles south of Honolulu. Colonists were rotated in and out of these barren islands, to maintain the US claim on them, and during the cruises *Taney* transported colonists and provisions for them, in cooperation with the governing entity, the US Department of the Interior. In this photo, Richard B. Black (*center*), from the Department of the Interior, poses with several colonists in front of the Government House on Canton Island. *Ketenheim collection*

Taney is anchored off an island in the Pacific around 1938. A boat is moored alongside the cutter, adjacent to the boarding ladder. The ship was painted overall white, with the upper part of the smokestack and the boot topping (the band around the hull along the waterline) finished in black. *US Coast Guard*

Following an agreement between the United States and Great Britain for the common use of the islands of Canton and Enderbury in the South Pacific Ocean for international aviation and communication, Secretary of the Interior Harold Ickes signed a license permitting Pan American Airways to use Canton Island as an air base for its commercial transpacific air transport service between California and New Zealand. Secretary Ickes is shown presenting the pen to Juan Trippe, president of Pan American, after the April 13, 1939, signing. *Library of Congress*

The cutter called at Hilo to load some canec [a fiberboard building material that was made from sugar cane] consigned to the American naval base at Pago Pago, the Samoan port having been added to the itinerary for this trip.

PAA's abandoned base at Pago Pago has been dismantled. Equipment will be transported by the *Taney* to Canton.

Several members of the ship's party spent most of their time ashore in Hilo in a drugstore purchasing trinkets to trade the natives in Samoa.

Sailed from Hilo at 4 p.m. Sunday May 20.

Movies every night, sometimes double headers. Films shown on the way south will be exchanged for new supply at Pago Pago.

Most of the pictures are of rather ancient vintage. Some of them the sailors have seen so often that they accurately anticipate the action and shout the heroine's lines before she can get to them herself.

Twice during the first two nights out[,] seas sprayed the quarterdeck and wet part of the audience. Sometimes the motion of the cutter causes the folding chairs to fall to port or starboard like rows of dominoes.

Today the seamen began construction of a tank in which all polliwogs (passengers and crew members who have not crossed the Equator) will be dunked as port of the line-crossing ceremonies.

May 28

Canton was sighted at 6 a.m., a thin, white strip of land off our port bow. Rain clouds hung low over the atoll as the sun rose from its slumbers to greet the *Taney*.

As the cutter approached the main entrance to the lagoon[,] landmarks became distinguishable, including the British and American flags which fly compatibly above the island.

June 11

Yesterday the *Taney* serviced Howland and Baker. Baker, normally surrounded by pounding surf which makes landing difficult and sometimes impossible, was in an unusually hospitable mood.

Because of its proximity to Howland (40 miles) and the consequent duplication of services performed by colonists on both islands, and because sea conditions which normally make landing difficult, the department of interior is contemplating abandonment of the Baker colony.

If the island is abandoned, the department will be giving up its nearest equatorial outpost.

Adding a touch of historical significance to the *Taney*'s call at Howland was inspection of Kamakaiwi Field by Robert Campbell, representative in Hawaii for the Civil Aeronautics authority.

In the prewar years, *Taney* sometimes was equipped with floatplanes, to assist with patrolling. The first such aircraft the Coast Guard employed aboard its ships was the Grumman JF-2, and *Taney* was the first USCG ship to embark the JF-2, in 1937. Here, the aircraft is suspended from a boom off the port side of the quarterdeck. *Ketenheim collection*

Mr. Campbell personally supervised construction of the airport on Howland in the spring of 1937 in anticipation of Amelia Earhart's flight from New Guinea.

Kamakaiwi Field, named after James Kamakaiwi, leader of the Howland colony at the time of the Earhart flight, is probably the world's only airport upon which a plane has not landed.

In stark contrast to the manner in which such information would be flowing in two years' time, the October 10, 1940, headlines of the *Honolulu Star-Advertiser* announced, "Cutter *Taney*'s Armament to Be Increased." The article went on, "Ship goes into Pearl Harbor to be Rearmed on return Oct. 25," then added the details that

> the Coast Guard cutter *Taney*, upon her return from her present cruise to the South Pacific, will go into the Pearl Harbor navy yard to be fitted with additional guns and other armament to fit her for naval use, it was learned yesterday.
>
> The *Taney* is in the American Line Islands on her quarterly supply replenishment cruise to the groups of colonists stationed in the South Pacific.

The article continued:

> The *Taney* will arrive in Honolulu about Oct. 25 and proceed to the navy yard, where the installation work will be completed.
>
> The work is being undertaken under the $8,098,660 appropriated by Congress for emergency conversion of Coast Guard vessels for naval use.
>
> Conversion work includes the revision of armament and ammunition stowage arrangements; installation of guns; enlargement of magazines; fitting of depth charge racks and "Y" guns; installation of underwater sound detection apparatus; and structural changes incident to these installations.

In fact, *Taney*'s entry into the Pearl Harbor Navy Yard was postponed until January 7, 1941, and it was expected that the work would be complete in early to mid-March.

On April 20, 1941, newspapers nationwide carried a United Press story with the headline announcing the transfer of the Treasury-class cutters to the Navy. The story read, in part,

> The Coast Guard is preparing some of its most powerful cutters for transfer to the Navy, it was reported reliably last night.

Movement of certain cutters to shipyards for "overhaul" was believed to preface actual induction of the Coast Guard craft into Navy duty.

The cutter *Roger B. Taney*, formerly stationed at Honolulu, was en route to San Francisco for an overhaul. Two other cutters of the *Taney*'s class were reported undergoing similar treatment in yards in New York and Philadelphia.

The Navy was expected to get seven of the Coast Guard's best sea-going cutters, all about 2,000 tons and launched in 1936 and 1937. The cutters to be transferred were believed to be the *Taney*, the *George W. Campbell*, the *Samuel D. Ingham*, the *William J. Duane*, the *Alexander Hamilton*, the *Johnson G. Spencer* and the *George M. Bibb*.

In April, *Taney* steamed for Mare Island for overhaul and modification. Upon arrival in California waters on April 29, *Taney* did not immediately go into the shipyard's drydock; rather, she tied up at Mare Island. This was fortuitous for yachtsman Frank Bilek, as the *Oakland Tribune* reported on May 4: "Directed by a Coast Guard plane to a yacht floating helplessly in San Pablo Bay, a crew from the Coast Guard Cutter Taney yesterday saved the lone occupant of the boat from possible death."

It was reported in the Washington, DC, *Evening Star* that "on May 7, the President placed fourteen seagoing cutters, and the Coast Guard's Hawaiian district, under Navy orders."

The May 9 issue of the *Virginian-Pilot* included a feature that began,

> Although they have been practically in the Navy for some months, seven of the Coast Guard's largest offshore cutters are to be taken over officially by the Navy Department within the next few days, it was announced yesterday in reports from Washington.
>
> The cutters are almost sister ships and are the newest additions to the service. They include the *Bibb* and *Hamilton*, of the Norfolk district, and the *Spencer*, *Ingham*, *Campbell*, *Taney*, and *Duane*.

While control of the ship was transferred to the Navy, *Taney* remained a US Coast Guard ship. Despite what many publications state, the archival records are clear that the ship was always listed as USCGC *Taney*—never USS *Taney*—and essentially all official correspondence flowed through the commandant of the Coast Guard's office.

On May 28, 1941, *Taney* was nearly lost—ironically while in Navy Yard, Mare Island. At about 7:00 a.m. that day, a fire broke out in the life-jacket-and-boat-gear locker of the ship as the result

The US Coast Guard also operated Curtiss SOC floatplanes in the late 1930s; an example is poised above the quarterdeck of *Taney* around 1939. The ship lacked a catapult; when a floatplane was embarked, it was stored on the quarterdeck, and a boom was used to lower the plane to the water for launching, and to recover it after landing on the surface of the ocean.

of welding being done on the overhead of the carpenter's shop below. While this began relatively small, soon the entire compartment was involved, drawing the attention of a tug alongside. Part of the work being done in the yard involved overhaul of the general alarm system, so it was nonfunctional. Likewise, because the ship was in the yard, the ship's fire mains were disabled. A number of CO_2 extinguishers were nearby, but few worked. Shouts from the ship alerted a Marine ashore, who then summoned the Mare Island Fire Department. At about the same time, the nearby tug rigged a hose to *Taney*, which along with the fire department quickly extinguished the blaze.

That same day, a board of investigation was convened to look into the fire, which imperiled the ship, and concluded their work the same day. However, the matter did not end there. On Friday, June 6, three days before *Taney* departed Mare Island, her CO, Cmdr. Louis B. Olson, wrote,

> The proceedings of this board are not approved for the following reasons:
> Some of the inconsistencies in the testimony are not sufficiently investigated.
> Many of the important facts in connection with the fire are [[AU: not?]] touched upon in the evidence nor [*sic*] mentioned in the findings, such as the fact that numerous CO_2 bottles were actually used on the fire, the fact that the crew fought the fire and extinguished it in time to contain all damage to the original space and save some of the material therein in spite of its highly inflammable nature. No report of the existence or absence of personal injury is made. Other material points are not covered.

Continuing, Olson wrote, "The findings of facts are substantially correct, except are incomplete in very many respects."

Capt. G. T. Finlay, USCG, commander of the Honolulu District (to which *Taney* was assigned), also had his misgivings, writing in part on June 30:

> The proceedings of this board are a record of testimony of witnesses which fails to elicit definite information on important phases of events which occurred prior to and subsequent to the discovery of fire on board the TANEY. After an incident of this kind, it is very easy to say what should have been done to prevent a fire, but it is very evident that thought was not given to such possible preventative steps in this particular case[,] and the board did not develop this angle in testimony nor was the subject of what firefighting equipment was immediately available.

On November 3, 1941, President Roosevelt signed an executive order transferring the Coast Guard to Navy control.

As the 1941 calendar turned to December, *Taney*, wearing a fresh Navy paint scheme rather than the bright white of the Coast Guard, was again in Hawaiian waters. In addition to resuming her former duties, she now alternated harbor entrance and channel antisubmarine patrol duties with the four vintage destroyers of Destroyer Division 80: *Allen* (DD-66), *Schley* (DD-103), *Chew* (DD-106), and *Ward* (DD-139).

Taney is moored alongside the US Coast Guard station at Pier 4, Honolulu, around 1940. Partway up the foremast was an enclosed crow's nest, which offered observers an elevated position that was protected from the elements. Also in view are the two 6-pounder saluting guns to the front of the pilothouse. *US Coast Guard*

Taney reported to the Navy Yard, Mare Island, California, in the spring of 1941 for repairs and modernization. A key part of this refitting was the installation of improved guns with 3-inch/50-caliber and 5-inch/51-caliber pieces, replacing the original 1-pounder and 6-pounder guns. The crews of these guns were protected by steel splinter shields. Other improvements included a new, armored pilothouse with portholes, and a searchlight platform on the foremast. Two depth-charge racks had been installed on the fantail; the rear of the rack on the port side is protruding from the rear of the bulwark. A few weeks after the refitting at Mare Island, where the ship is shown, *Taney* was transferred to the operational control of the US Navy in late 1941. *Ketenheim collection*

CHAPTER 3
Taney in World War II

As *Taney* was tied up at her usual mooring of Pier 6 in Honolulu Harbor on the morning of December 7, 1941, at 0645 her antisubmarine patrol colleague *Ward* made history by attacking a Japanese Ko-hyoteki-class, two-man midget submarine that was attempting to follow the cargo ship *Antares* into Pearl Harbor.

Taney, which was on two-hour standby, was informed shortly thereafter. The ship had been scheduled for gunnery practice Monday morning, and in preparation her ready service boxes had been filled on Saturday evening.

The ship's after-action report concerning December 7 and the days immediately following records:

To: Commandant, 14th Naval District

Subject: Taney; report of activities Dec. 7–20, 1941

Reference: (a) Article 712, US Navy regulations

1) When anti-aircraft fire was first observed over Pearl Harbor on Dec. 7th, general quarters were sounded, and all officers not on board ordered to return. The anti-aircraft battery—as well as all other guns—were ready to fire with their full crew and three officers at their stations within four minutes. The remaining officers—with one exception—were aboard less than 10 minutes later.

Steam was ordered and [the] vessel was ready to get underway. Without having received orders from any source, between 0901 and 0902 and between 0915 and 0918 opened fire on scattering formations of enemy aircraft at a high altitude passing over the harbor from west to east, using #4 and #5 3" guns. #3 gun did not bear, and machine guns were outranged. Long fuse settings were used, but fire failed to reach [the] planes. 27 rounds of 3" shrapnel were fired in these attacks. At 1135, opened fire with 3" gun on a small formation of enemy planes which passed over the city from north to south and were almost overhead at [the] time of firing. One of these planes appeared to have dropped a bomb on Sand Island. No report was heard, but dust and smoke were observed. At 1158, a formation of five enemy planes approached the vessel directly from the south[-]southwest over the harbor entrance on what appeared to be a glide bombing or strafing attack on this vessel or more probably a bombing attack on the power plant which is located north of [the] vessel's berth at Pier 6, Honolulu.

Fire was opened with #4 and #5 3" guns, and #3, #4, #5, and #6 .50/Cal. Machine guns after planes were in range. No direct hits by the 3" guns were definitely seen, but planes were rocked by the fire and swerved up and away. Several 50/Cal. Tracers appeared to pierce [the] wing and tail structure of one plane. No bombs or machine gun bullets were received aboard, nor [sic] observed falling nearby.

54 rounds of 3" shrapnel were expended, and about 250 rounds of .50/Cal. Ammunition. The only casualty was a delay in firing #4 gun due to the projectile being unseated from [the] cartridge. [The] cartridge was rammed home, breech closed, and gun fired. A fairly satisfactory volume of fire was obtained, but it was not as great as would have been desirable, due to interference with loading from splinter shielding at that particular angle of fire.

A modification of the drill requiring an extra shell man was made and eliminates this difficulty. This vessel had had no opportunity to fire anti-aircraft practice, although the difficulty would not have appeared and might not have been discovered at the angles of fire used in prescribed practices.

The officers and crew bore themselves well, although most members of the crew had had no training except drill and had never seen anything above a .50 caliber fired.

2) Proceeded to sea at 0546, 8 December, and commenced patrol of vicinity of Honolulu Harbor entrance. On this patrol, made sound contact with submarines and dropped depth charges as listed below:

Position	Time	No. Dropped	Result
About 3 miles SE of Ahoa Pt.	1230, Dec. 8	3	Unknown
1.2 miles 207 degrees from #1 buoy	0200, Dec. 10	2	Unknown
3 miles 183 degrees from Aloha Tower	2043, Dec. 10	3	Oil slick observed
4 miles 126 degrees from #1 buoy	1703, Dec. 11	6	Unknown
4 miles 120 degrees from #1 buoy	1702, Dec. 11	2	Unknown
2.7 miles 200 degrees from Aloha Tower	1500, Dec. 13	3	Unknown
3.5 miles 206 degrees from Aloha Tower	040, Dec. 14	5	Unknown

In April and May 1942, *Taney* underwent modernization and refitting at the Navy Yard, Pearl Harbor, to prepare the ship for convoy-escort duty. Radar was installed on the ship, and several crewmen received training in operating the radar. A stateroom previously used by the force commander was converted to a radar room. This view off the port bow was taken during that refitting. In the foreground is the raised bulwark around the forecastle, a modification added several years before. Farther aft are the anchor chains and combination wildcats and capstans. The wildcats are wheels that transfer power from the windlass motor belowdecks to the anchor chains. The capstans, above the wildcats, are used mainly for operating mooring lines. Next aft are the forward 3-inch/50-caliber gun and the forward 5-inch/51-caliber gun, to the upper rear of which is another 3-inch/50-caliber gun. The USCG white paint had been painted over in a USN "graded" camouflage (of more than one color: note the change in color on the bulwark along the forecastle). The camouflage seems to have been Measure 12, with vertical surfaces finished in Sea Blue (5-S) from the waterline to the level of the main deck, Ocean Gray (5-O) from the main deck to the top of the smokestack, and Haze Gray (5-H) on surfaces above the smokestack. *Ketenheim collection*

3) Approaches were made in as close adherence to doctrine as possible. Visible results were disappointing, except in the case described in detail below. The following characteristics were common to most contacts:

(a) True bearing changed little if at all after [the] vessel brought contact dead ahead. This might indicate a wake knuckle or a former depth charge disturbance, and in some cases, this was probably true, but it is believed in most cases it meant that [the] enemy was proceeding directly toward or away from [the] vessel. The approaches indicated this particularly in two cases where the range decreased very slowly in one case and very rapidly in another.

(b) All contacts were made at short ranges—800 yards or less—indicating the possibility that the target was considerably smaller than submarines on which practice had been conducted when contacts of 1,500–2,000 yards had been made. With this type of contact, the probability of false contacts with wake knuckles and large fish is increased. One very large manta badly injured was observed at one time, and a slightly smaller one floating dead was observed later. These fish may have been accidentally injured or killed, but it is possible that they were actually targets for some attacks, not necessarily by this vessel.

c) Difficulty was experienced in regaining contact after an attack. Search around the disturbed area of the first attack was usually useless, possibly because submarine had succeeded in getting out of effective range (less than 800 yards.)

3) Description of three attacks follows:

2045, 10 December 1941. This contact developed shortly after tracer bullets over the vicinity of the harbor entrance were observed ahead, apparently aimed at a surface vessel, although none could be observed from this vessel. Sound contact was made on the starboard bow shortly thereafter, and [the] vessel made an approach beginning with a sharp turn to starboard to bring submarine ahead.

Rate of change of range indicated that [the] submarine was running away. Completed approach and dropped three charges with 100[-]yard spread. Immediately after attack, turned right and attempted to regain contact. Returning echo indicated possible contact almost dead ahead and in vicinity of our first turn. Signaled Ramsay patrolling with us and approaching that spot to search, but her search was without result.

The wake knuckle of our first turn may've produced the second echo. A thorough sound search of vicinity failed to re-establish contact. A very strong odor of fuel oil was noticed aft after the attack and the turn down wind. For several hours, this odor was noticeable when passing this spot, diminishing toward morning. A definite oil slick persisted in this spot for two days. In smooth water, it was not observed after that time. On two separate days thereafter, with high winds and quite choppy seas, a clearly defined oil slick—50–100 yards in diameter—was observed ¾-mile–one mile to leeward.

Since depth of [the] water was over 200 fathoms and under these wind conditions a current of one knot and a half develops here; it is possible that this slick might have come from [the] same source.

1703, 11 December 1941. Dropped six charges using Y gun on an urgent approach at full speed on a sound contact made while a cruiser was leaving Pearl Harbor and within torpedo range.

0940, 14 December 1941. Dropped five charges on an excellent contact with range closing fast from dead ahead. This was the best contact made, solid and definite, and all hands were convinced that results would be obtained, but no visible evidence of damage to [the] submarine was found. A careful search of [the] vicinity failed to re-establish contact.

In a view from off the port quarter of *Taney* at Pearl Harbor in April or May 1942, the previously installed depth-charge racks are in the foreground, loaded with twelve depth charges each. During this refitting, to supplement these depth-charge racks, depth-charge projectors, which propelled the depth charges outward, were installed on the main deck amidships. On the quarterdeck are the aft 5-inch/51-caliber gun and its splinter shield. On the rear of the superstructure, at the 01 level, are the two aft 3-inch/50-caliber gun mounts, equipped with splinter shields. *Ketenheim collection*

The air-search radar antenna installed on *Taney* in the spring of 1942 is visible at the top of the foremast in this June 1942 photograph. Mounted on a pedestal above the pilothouse is a platform for the director for the guns, which was part of the fire-control system. Life rafts are stored on the side of the superstructure.

In a June 1942 photo taken from the forecastle of *Taney*, the forward 3-inch/50-caliber gun is trained to starboard, while just aft of it the forward 5-inch/51-caliber gun is trained forward. Fire hoses are stored on the front of the splinter shield of the 3-inch piece. To each side of the pilothouse is a searchlight.

As seen from the searchlight platform on the foremast, members of the crew of the director in the foreground are training the device to port, in unison with the 5-inch and 3-inch guns below, which also are trained to port. The photo was taken in June 1942, during which month *Taney* engaged in searching for survivors of the Battle of Midway.

4) After considerable thought on this subject as a result of previous sound training practices, a study of the doctrine and the experiences of this period, a changed method of estimating an approach when contact develops at close range has been worked out and will be submitted in a separate letter as a possible improvement.

L. B. Olson

Copy to:

COMDESDIV 80

SCG014NAVDIST

File.

Confidential

It was during this time that *Taney* received the hull classification WPG-37. On January 22, 1942, *Taney* steamed from Pearl Harbor on a Line Island cruise that was vastly different from the many such cruises she had made previously. On this voyage she was escorting the freighter SS *Barbara Olson*, and the duo arrived at Canton Island on January 28, where *Taney*'s men were detailed to unload barrels of aviation gas from the freighter.

From Canton the ships steamed to Enderbury Island, where the four colonists were taken aboard at 1015 on February 7, and then turned her guns on the structures on Enderbury. Moving to Jarvis Island, she again removed the colonists before setting fire to the structures of the Island. *Taney*, along with *Barbara Olson*, steamed to Palmyra, arriving on February 12, where additional cargo was unloaded at the naval air station.

Taney arrived back at Honolulu on March 5 and, just over a month later, entered the Pearl Harbor shipyard for modification. Her Browning machine guns were replaced with more-powerful 20 mm weapons, her #2 5-inch gun, suitable only for surface engagements, was replaced with a 3-inch dual-purpose gun, an updated radar suite was installed, and smoke generators as well as large depth charge racks were installed at her stern. This work was completed in May, and the following month *Taney* steamed for Midway, taking supplies to the island and searching for survivors of the epic sea battle that bore the atoll's name. During a second such trip, the enemy launched a torpedo attack on *Taney*, which fortunately was unsuccessful. Also fortunate, during one of these voyages Coxswain Clifford K. Johnson fell overboard at night while *Taney* was steaming to Midway. Miraculously, his cries for help were heard by the crew of the seaplane tender USS *Wright* (AV-1), who were able to locate him by using one of the ship's spotlights and then dispatch a boat for the otherwise doomed Johnson.

Taney evaded enemy bombs in July 1943, when sharp maneuvering prevented bombs from a Japanese Mavis from finding their mark on the cutter, which then was taking a survey party to Baker Island in order to establish an emergency landing strip. Fearing that additional aircraft would join in the attack, the ship put into Palmyra, resuming the mission to Baker Island later in the month.

The winter of 1943 saw *Taney* returning to the mainland, steaming to Mare Island Navy Yard, Vallejo, California, for overhaul and refit—availability in Navy parlance. Her armament was completely revised, with four 5-inch single enclosed mounts being installed, two forward and two aft, and her 20 mm battery being reconfigured. *Taney* was the only Treasury-class cutter to be fitted with this main battery configuration.

Her postavailability trials completed, *Taney* pointed her bow toward Atlantic waters for the first time since her initial operations. After transiting the Panama Canal, the men of *Taney* reported that the ship was being trailed by a German U-boat, a situation that would continue for five days. Ultimately, *Taney* arrived in Boston, entering the Navy Yard there on March 14 for further modification—notably the installation of a new Combat Information Center (CIC) and installation of a new type of steering gear. With the yard work completed on March 29, *Taney* steamed south to Hampton Roads, where she arrived on March 31. On April 2, she departed Norfolk as flagship of Task Force (TF) 66 and convoy guide for convoy UGS-38. Much of the operation was routine, as denoted in the ship's war diary, which reads as follows:

> 1. USCGC TANEY is a unit of TASK FORCE 66, U.S. Atlantic Fleet on 2 April 1944 and operating under Commander TASK FORCE 66 OPERATION ORDER NO. 1-44 dated 2 April 1944. Commander TASK FORCE 66, Captain W. H. Duvall, USN in this vessel.
>
> 2. Operations were essentially the same during the period of this report and are therefore covered in one letter. TASK FORCE 66 engaged in escorting convoy UGS 38.
>
> The convoy made about 9.5 knots for most of the journey, and the War Diary notes for April 22, "Task Force 66 relieved of escort of UGS 38 by British escort off Bizerte, North Africa at 0815 B. Maneuvered off entrance and then proceeded to enter port. At 1404 secured to fuel docks at Bizerte, North Africa in company with other units of TASK FORCE 66.
>
> 23 April 1944 to 30 April 1944. At Bizerte, North Africa throughout. Operations uneventful.

Indeed, the period at Bizerte was uneventful; however, the voyage there was considerably more hazardous than the war diary reflects. Just more than a half hour after sunset on April 13, not long after the convoy made landfall of the Azores, the convoy came under aerial attack from the Germans. Flying low so that Allied radar could not distinguish them from the shoreline, Junkers Ju 88s and Heinkel He 111s came at the convoy in three waves. Striking from dead ahead, the first wave succeeded in torpedoing *Paul Hamilton* and *Samite*. *Hamilton*, laden with ammunition, blew up in a tremendous explosion, killing all 580 men on board instantly, including 154 officers and men of the 831st Bombardment Squadron and 317 officers and men of the 32nd Photo Reconnaissance Squadron.

Two more ships, *Stephen F. Austin* and *Royal Star*, were hit by the second wave, with two torpedoes churning past *Taney* close aboard. The third wave hit the Benson-class destroyer *Lansdale* (DD-426). The ship was listing heavily and mortally wounded, and her captain ordered her abandoned. Five minutes later she broke in half, with the stern portion sinking immediately, and the

As viewed from the main deck near the forward port corner of the superstructure in June 1942, the forward 3-inch/51-caliber gun and crew are in the foreground, to the front of the pilothouse. Above and aft is the director.

On a platform with a round splinter shield on the quarterdeck in another June 1942 photo is the aft 5-inch/50-caliber gun, with the crew at their stations by the mount. Farther forward are the two aft 3-inch/51-caliber guns, in side-by-side mounts on the 01 level of the deckhouse. Above and forward of the 3-inch guns are four 20 mm guns, two per side, with gun shields and splinter shields.

remainder twenty minutes later. Forty-seven of her officers and men perished.

Taney and the rest of Task Force 66 left Bizerte on May 1 and, but for a suspected U-boat contact on May 5, had an uneventful crossing to New York. Her war diary did note, however, that "echo[-]ranging conditions in Mediterranean Sea were very poor due to water layers. The foxer equipment issued to this vessel was deficient in that all carried away in normal operation. The towline between the depressor and foxer gear parted each time. Each parting was different place and occurred within minutes or less than 4 hours. Four equipments carried away. Type Mark II complete with towline."

Taney entered Ambrose Channel, New York, at 1255 on May 21 and entered Navy Yard, New York, for availability the next day. This yard period lasted until June 7.

The next day, *Taney* steamed into Gravesend Bay, off Long Island, to take on ammunition, prior to steaming for Hampton Roads, conducting firing exercises at various points along the way. Aboard was Capt. W. H. Duvall, commander of Task Force 66.

On June 12, *Taney* put to sea as the flagship of convoy UGS-45. The convoy passed through the Straits of Gibraltar on June 27, and the next day a portion of the convoy split off, bound for Oran. That same day, the escorts laid smoke around the convoy, which was thirteen columns wide, during the dusk alert. The process was repeated during the dawn and dusk alerts the next day as well, and during the dawn alert on June 30, at which time the convoy reformed in three columns. They reached Bizerte the next day.

Taney remained moored at Pier A, Infirmary Point, Karouba, Tunisia, until July 10, when she left and became the flagship of the returning convoy, designated GUS-45. *Taney* and her charges arrived at Point Zebra off New York at 1843 on July 28 and arrived at the Navy Yard in Brooklyn at 2244. She began an availability the next day, which was not completed until August 3, at which time she took aboard ammunition at Gravesend Bay and began steaming toward Casco Bay, Maine. She would remain in Casco Bay conducting training exercises until the morning of August 18, when she steamed for Hampton Roads, entering Chesapeake Bay the next day and tying up at the Naval Operating Base, Norfolk, at 1705.

Taney steamed out of the base and anchored in Lynnhaven Roads on August 22; the next day, *Taney*, along with the other escorts and convoy USB 52, began steaming once more toward Bizerte. Once again, *Taney* was the flagship of Capt. W. H. Duvall, commander of Task Force 66. *Taney* and her charges arrived at the North African port on September 11.

The cutter and the returning convoy, which was designated GUS 52, departed for America on September 18. *Taney* passed the Ambrose light on October 7, and *Taney* proceeded to the New York Navy Yard. The next day, Capt. Duvall transferred his flag to USS *Selfridge*, and *Taney* was detached from Task Force 66, ending her Atlantic convoy duties.

On October 9, *Taney* departed the New York Navy Yard bound for the Boston Navy Yard, South Annex, arriving the next day. On October 11, she was taken into the Navy Yard, and work began to convert *Taney* to an AGC (Amphibious Group Command ship), which would take the remainder of the year. This conversion, preparations for which had begun on August 12, included adding accommodations for an embarked flag officer and his staff, as well as increased communications and radar facilities, and resulted in her hull classification being changed to WAGC-37. Her armament was modified as well, with the four enclosed mounts giving way to two open-mount 5-inch guns, and for the first time a trio of twin 40 mm Bofors antiaircraft guns as well as four 20 mm guns.

The conversion work was extensive, and the conversion itself was plagued with problems, such that an acrimonious relationship developed between *Taney*'s captain, Cmdr. George D. Synon, and the Boston Navy Yard.

On January 2, 1945, Synon submitted a six-page progress report to the commander of Amphibious Training Command regarding the situation, concerning work done during the week ending December 30, saying,

1. The USCGC Taney is undergoing conversion to AGC at the South Boston Drydock, Navy Yard, Boston, Mass.

2. The Taney arrived in the Navy Yard on October 10, 1944. Eighty-seven (87) days navy yard availability were granted, and the completion date is January 5, 1945. Five (5) days readiness for sea have been authorized.

3. The Production and Planning Officers assure that all repairs will be accomplished by the completion date.

4. It is assured, likewise, that all authorized alterations will be completed.

5. The commanding officer regard the general situation with respect to timely completion as unfavorable. After careful observation of the rate and progress of the work throughout the entire period the ship has been in the yard, he is convinced she cannot be placed in acceptable condition by midnight of January 5. Moreover, governing military items cannot even be completed by this time. This conclusion has been reached after consultation with Navy Yard officers and employees in immediate charge of the work and through critical inspections by the ship's officers. The production officer has advised the commanding officer that it may be necessary to use the ship's readiness for sea period for the completion of work that otherwise would not be accomplished. If so, the efficiency with which the ship can be prepared for sea will depend upon the degree to which the crew is hampered by the presence of Yard workmen on board. It is desired to point out that this ship has been practically out of commission for three months. Every item of stores, ammunition and portable equipment must be returned and stowed on the ship. In addition, a sea trial must be accomplished and various tests and calibrations made. It is a job that requires the total energy and attention of all hands. If, in addition, the Navy Yard workmen (and women) are simultaneously to be employed in the ship the interference and distraction offered to the crew will be considerable.

This strongly worded introduction was followed by an almost three-page list of work remaining to be done, followed by a critique of the work that had been done, the opening passages of which are reproduced below:

Three of the 20 mm guns seen in the preceding photo are viewed from a closer perspective in June 1942. Some of the gun crewmen are sitting on the splinter shields. On the front of the foremast is the searchlight platform, below which is the director. Both of these features are equipped with canvas windbreaks.

A Douglas A-20 Havoc is zooming past the port side of *Taney* sometime in June 1942. Six 20 mm mounts are visible, three on each side of the smokestack, with the guns having been removed from three of the mounts. The 20 mm guns that are mounted are at maximum elevation, with canvas weather covers fitted over them.

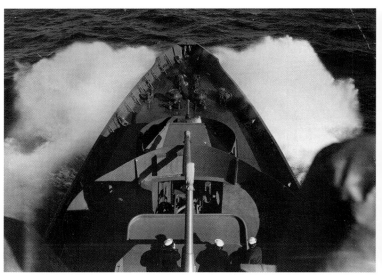

The bow of *Taney* crashes through a swell during a patrol in June 1942. The muzzles of the three forward guns are fitted with fabric covers.

The quality of the work accomplished to date, with few exceptions, has been very good. At this time, however, all trades are working under pressure and the deterioration in the quality of the output is noticeable. Particularly is this so with respect to the paint job. The exterior of the ship was scaled down to bare metal by the crew after many long hours of work with hand scrapers[,] and it was hoped that a good paint job would be obtained. Instead, the major part of the exterior surfaces was painted in temperatures well below freezing. Areas encrusted with ice were even painted. Much trouble was experienced in keeping paint off gaskets and fittings. This paint job is expected to be a source of grief for a long time to come. Some comment is believed indicated with respect to the treatment given sheet metal furniture and equipment by the yard workmen. Much of it is new and of excellent quality. It is discouraging to see it battered and abused before it is ever placed in service. Complaints in this connection have been met with the assurance that all damages will be repaired prior to the departure of the ship. The expansion joint installed in the deck house is not satisfactory. The open side is forward, instead of aft. The plating in the vicinity of the slip joint on the top side has not been straightened and the joint will leak excessively.

Cmdr. Synon's report was not well received by officials at Navy Yard, Boston, when they become aware of it. While a copy of their reply has not yet been located, we do have a copy of Synon's response, a portion of which appears below:

1. Paragraph 1 of reference (a) (the Navy Yard response) contains the comments of the Commandant, Navy Yard, Boston, with respect to the report made by the Commanding Officer, TANEY, in reference (b) (the January 2 letter above) that "The Production and Planning Officers assure that all repairs will be accomplished by the completion date." Inasmuch as these comments appear to touch upon the sincerity, if not the integrity, of the Commanding Officer in the submission of reference (b), he feels impelled to state, in accurate terms, the information which was available to him at the time of preparation of reference (b).

2. Excerpts from the Navy Yard endorsements to the Weekly Progress Reports follow:

Endorsement dated 16 December 1944: "The Yard expects to compete the subject vessel as scheduled.

Endorsement dated 20 December 1944: "Although there is considerable work remaining on the subject vessel[,] the Navy Yard expects to complete as scheduled."

Endorsement dated 29 December 1944: "The delay (caused by cold weather) has not been sufficient to warrant a new completion date."

3. No correspondence received by this ship has contained any statement by the Navy Yard to the effect that an extension of availability might be required.

4. On 2 January, the Commanding Officer reported in person to the Production Officer that the work was not sufficiently advanced to warrant readiness for sea preparations, such as taking ammunition, fuel, and stores, to commence as scheduled. At this time the Production Officer informed the Commanding Officer that the ship would be ready as scheduled if he, the Commanding Officer, would "pitch in." On 3 January, in the handwriting of the Production Officer, the Commanding Officer was informed that "the schedule of fueling during Yard availability and taking ammunition immediately after Yard availability, 6 Jan., should be adhered to for present." Reference (b) was not released until after the receipt of this last communication.

On January 4, 1945, Coast Guard Headquarters in Washington confirmed the change in hull classification to the chief of naval operations via a coded message reading, "To CNO. Your official designation is USCGC Taney. Visual Call W 3 7. 37 should be printed on bows. Type classification AGC."

On January 7, 1945, *Taney*'s availability was extended from January 5 to midnight on January 9, and readiness for sea was extended to January 14.

On January 10, 1945, *Taney* left the Navy Yard, venturing into Massachusetts Bay to undergo power drills, test backing power and rudder response, and perform a rough magnetic compass adjustment—all of which were satisfactory. The returned to Pier 2 at the Boston Navy Yard.

As it happened, even with the extension there was not enough time, since a coded message of January 10 stated, "USCGC Taney completion will be further delayed until midnight 12 Jan. due [to] large volume additional work developed during testing period following extensive conversion."

Taney took aboard a full load of ammunition on January 11, and the remaining stores, supplies, and spares were loaded on January 18. That same day, the officers and crew moved back aboard, along with three officers and twenty-three men of her Marine Corps detachment. At 2330 she got underway, bound for Norfolk for ten days of shakedown training as part of Task Force 20.

However, it seems that even then, much more work remained. On January 21, Cmdr. Synon wrote to the chief of naval operations, via the commander of Amphibious Training Command and the commandant of Navy Yard, Boston, a five-page message with this subject: "USCGC Taney; additional unsatisfactory work performed at NYdBox."

As a result, *Taney* was granted a four-day availability at Norfolk Navy Yard to repair the deficiencies. This also elicited a scathing message from the commander of Amphibious Training Command to the chief of naval operations, sharing Synon's "USCGC Taney; additional unsatisfactory work performed at NYdBox" subject line. That amphibious message reads, in part,

> This command notes, with concern, the unsatisfactory material condition of this vessel upon completion of the conversion.
>
> Notwithstanding the fact that two (2) extensions of availability and two (2) extensions of the readiness for sea period were granted, this vessel reported in a material condition necessitating the granting of a four (4) day availability in this area in order to place the vessel in a satisfactory condition of material readiness for onward routing.
>
> Vessels of this class are granted only ten (10) days for shakedown. This period includes the time required for transit from the conversion yard to the Hampton Roads Area. Therefore, the necessity for an availability to correct uncompleted or unsatisfactory conversion items results in a serious curtailment of the time available for essential training.
>
> It is desired to call attention to this matter in order to prevent a recurrence of the conditions reported in the basic letter.

Taney, in concert with a handful of other vessels, left Hampton Roads as Task Unit 29.6.3 on January 29, bound once more for Pacific waters. The task unit reached Panama on February 3, anchoring at Cristóbal. The next afternoon, they proceeded to the canal, passing on February 5. At 1619 that day, SS *Pocket Canyon* collided with the moored *Taney*, damaging a 40 mm splinter shield, muzzle flash hider, and radio antenna, all at starboard aft. At 1752 she departed alone from Balboa, bound for San Diego.

Taney put into Naval Repair Base San Diego for minor repair on February 13. The repairs were completed on February 15, and on the sixteenth she set course for Pearl Harbor, which she reached on February 22.

During this time, the commander, administrative command, Amphibious Forces, US Pacific Fleet, conducted a study of *Taney* "to determine its capabilities with respect to officer and crew accommodations in view of the prospective use of this class as flag ships." The study concluded that in its then-present form, *Taney* could accommodate seventy-two officers, twenty-four CPOs, and 240 enlisted men, and that minor changes could increase the enlisted men's accommodations by sixteen bunks. If the recommended change was made, and after deducting the space required for the ship's crew, there would remain these accommodations for flag officers and personnel—forty-two officers, one CPO, and thirty enlisted men.

The study went on to note, "It is a physical impossibility to provide berthing for additional men within the existing superstructure and general arrangement. The stability of the ship is critical and prohibits the additional of superstructure compartments."

March 1 found *Taney* moored at Berth S-19, undergoing minor repairs and installation of additional communications equipment. On March 6, the flag of RAdm. Calvin H. Cobb was hoisted, and he and his staff came aboard. Four days later, *Taney* got underway for Eniwetok, which was reached on March 18. The next day she was at sea again, steaming toward Ulithi, where she arrived on the twenty-third, dropping anchor at the Arishi Anchorage, where she would remain until April 7.

At 0610, *Taney* and numerous other ships left Ulithi bound for Okinawa, where she anchored in Berth H-160 on April 11. She shifted berths to H-46 on April 15. During *Taney*'s first forty-five days at Okinawa, her crew went to general quarters 119 times! During the same period, her crew was credited with shooting down four enemy aircraft and assisting in the downing of several more. This was especially significant considering the high number of kamikaze attacks launched against the Allied ships in the waters off Okinawa. Tragically, on May 21, *Taney* also downed a US F6F Hellcat, which was approaching the ship during a time when the fleet had been advised that no friendly aircraft were in the area, and the ship was under orders to engage any aircraft encountered.

Life aboard *Taney* was difficult due to the frequent alerts, hot temperatures, and constant threat of attack, but the men fell into a routine. That routine was disrupted on August 1, when she got underway from Buckner Bay and put to sea in accordance with the navy's typhoon plan, escorting other ships that had the vessels steam in a crude boxlike course out of the typhoon's path and back to Buckner Bay on August 3.

On August 15 (Japan time; August 14, North American time), it was announced that the Japanese had agreed to surrender. For *Taney*'s crew, the war was over.

In July 1943, while *Taney* was on a mission to Baker Island, south of Honolulu and near the equator, a Japanese Kawanishi H6K "Mavis" flying boat spotted the ship and approached it. As seen in this photo, crews of the aft 3-inch/50-caliber gun and the 20 mm guns to the port side of the smokestack are firing their pieces at the Mavis while the crew of the aft 5-inch/51-caliber gun in the foreground observe the firing. *Ketenheim collection*

On its second pass over *Taney*, the Mavis dropped several bombs, none of which hit the target, owing to the decision of the ship's commanding officer, Capt. Perkins, to execute a sharp turn to port when the bombs were released. Crewmen of *Taney* are looking skyward in the aftermath of the bombing run; in the center background is the wake caused by a bomb striking the water. *Ketenheim collection*

After the crew of the Mavis discovered *Taney*'s location, the ship reversed its course and made its way to Palmyra Island, north of the Equator, where it dropped anchor in the lagoon to enable the crew to regroup. In a view taken at Palmyra, the depth-charge racks on the fantail are fully loaded. The ship's number, "37," is visible on the bow.

A landing party is preparing to disembark from *Taney* off Baker Island on July 25, 1943, to survey the island for an airfield. The personnel are wearing life jackets and steel helmets, and, as a normal security precaution, they are armed with rifles and bayonets.

In another photo of the landing party prior to landing on Baker Island, the island is faintly visible as a white line on the horizon. Toward the upper left is the breech of the starboard aft 3-inch/50-caliber gun.

On the quarterdeck just aft of the 5-inch/51-caliber gun, a crewman of *Taney* is test-firing a Browning Automatic Rifle, during July 1943. This evidently was at the time of the Baker Island landing.

A boat containing an armed landing party is being towed by a motorized boat toward shore at Baker Island on July 25, 1943, as *Taney* stands by in the background.

The boat with the portion of the landing party that was first ashore at Baker Island is being prepared for the final approach to the shore. A crewman aboard the boat is adjusting the tow rope.

A boat with part of the landing party is approaching the westerly shore of Baker Island. Trailing from the boat is a COIR line, the other end of which was moored to a station boat that was anchored close to the shore. A lightweight rope made from coconut husks, COIR line floated on water, which helped prevent it from getting snagged in submerged coral reefs. The line would be used to tow the boat and occupants quickly offshore if the need arose.

As photographed from a station boat, another boat has just delivered one-half of the armed landing party to Baker Island. Several members have advanced as skirmishers toward the sand dune in the background, while others are hunkered in the surf or are still in the boat. The landing boat was a self-bailer, which was able to discharge water automatically from the hull.

A photographer snapped this view from inside a landing boat at Baker Island, while members of the party disembarked and moved forward. The coast guardsman in the foreground to the right has a corpsman's red cross on his sleeve.

Men are hauling on a line to bring one of the landing boats ashore at Baker Island on July 25, 1943. Farther out is an anchored station boat, while in the distance is *Taney*.

The men hauling the boat to shore are viewed from a different perspective.

Members of the landing party pose for a photo next to the colors, on Baker Island. Crates with survey gear are to the rear of the men. The coast guardsman to the left is holding an M1 carbine, while the one to the right is armed with a Thompson machine gun.

A signalman on the beach at Baker Island is using flags to send a message to *Taney* or the station boat anchored offshore.

Faintly visible in the background of another photo of part of the landing team are some of the structures previously built on Baker Island for colonization purposes, as well as the lighthouse, in the distance to the right of the US flag.

TANEY IN WORLD WAR II 39

A member of the landing party stands in the doorway of the Baker Island lighthouse on July 25, 1943. The structure exhibits pockmarks and damage incurred during previous Japanese aerial attacks.

The US Department of the Interior maintained facilities for colonists on Baker Island prior to the war. Two men from *Taney*'s landing party are standing over the ruins of a root cellar, damaged in a Japanese attack.

This shed previously was used to shelter drums of potable water on Baker Island. Japanese aircraft strafed the shed during one of their attacks, puncturing many of the drums.

The survey party that was landed from Taney goes about its work of verifying the feasibility of locating an airfield on Baker Island. The results of the survey were favorable, and later that summer a construction team built an airfield capable of handling aircraft as large as B-24 Liberators, in support of the invasion of Tarawa.

The survey team retrieved this wooden grave marker on Baker Island in July 1943; it was photographed on the deck of Taney. Several names are carved on the marker, along with a cross at the top and "Baker Island" toward the bottom.

Four members of the survey party stand on the beach, awaiting a ride back to Taney, lying offshore in the distance.

The Hedgehog projector is at the center of the photo. The base of this antisubmarine device held twenty-four steel rods called spigots, upon which the hollow bases of the depth bombs were inserted. The projectiles were fired toward the front of the ship and had fuses that detonated by contact or barometric pressure. On the rear of the Hedgehog projector is a blast shield. To the rear of the Hedgehog and on the main deck forward of the Hedgehog are openings for where the foundations for the new 5-inch gun mounts will be installed.

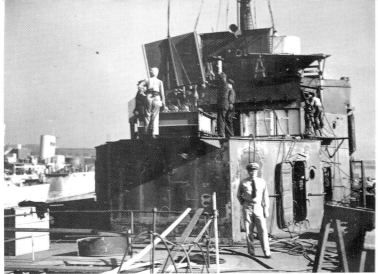

Taney proceeded to the Navy Yard, Mare Island, California, in late 1943 for a round of modernizations, principally to her weapons, to prepare her for the role of a convoy escort. As seen from the foredeck, the forward end of the superstructure was modified: the 5-inch/51-caliber gun, the 3-inch/50-caliber gun, and their splinter shields were removed, to make way for two enclosed 5-inch/38-caliber dual-purpose guns (capable of taking on surface and aerial targets) and a "Hedgehog" depth-bomb projector. The new gun mounts are not yet present, but the Hedgehog is being installed on the roof of the first level of the superstructure.

The Hedgehog projector and the opening for the foundation of 5-inch/38-caliber gun mount number 2 are seen from the forward port quarter. On the side of the superstructure below the Hedgehog, the forward door opening has been plugged with a steel plate. Also, the front of the superstructure one level above the main deck has been altered, moved aft to provide clearance for the new 5-inch gun mount.

Alterations to the foredeck and the forward part of the superstructure are observed from the port side. The filled-in forward door on the first level of the superstructure is evident. The dark-colored steel plate on the side of the first level of the superstructure, aft of the future location of the new 5-inch gun mount number 2, represents the filling in of an indentation in the superstructure, as built.

Details of the altered front of the second level of the superstructure of *Taney* are shown. The removal of the front of the superstructure at the 01 level eliminated a crew shelter and an ammunition storage room to the front of the captain's cabin. A new bulwark with a wind deflector at the top has been installed the next level up, to the front of the pilothouse. The director platform and pedestal have been removed from the deck about the pilothouse.

The changes that are underway on the bridge to the front of the pilothouse are viewed close-up, including the new forward bulwark. On the front of the top level of the superstructure, below the loudspeaker, is a dark-colored, rectangular feature, which appears to be a concentration dial, also called a range clock, a device for visually transmitting range information from the director to the gun crews. This device would be removed during this modernization.

The searchlight platform would remain on the front of the foremast. The light-colored windscreens on the level above the pilothouse will soon be replaced by curved, metal bulwarks.

The superstructure and the smokestack of *Taney* are viewed from the port side during the modernization that lasted from late 1943 to early 1944 at Mare Island. The photo was taken around the same time as the preceding photos. The 20 mm gun mounts had been removed from the wing bridges to the sides of the pilothouse and from the platform just aft of the smokestack.

In a photo taken above the quarterdeck, facing forward, in late 1943, the platforms for the aft 3-inch and 5-inch gun mounts have been removed. During this refitting, the deckhouse (the narrower structure extending aft of the superstructure) would be extended aft, and it would support 5-inch/38-caliber gun mount number 3.

By the time this photo was taken in January 1944, the modernization of *Taney* at Mare Island was nearing completion. The four new single 5-inch/38-caliber gun mounts had been installed. These were termed "mounts" in lieu of turrets" and were installed in armored shields offering all-around protection to the crews and the vital parts of the guns. Also in view are the alterations to the forward part of the superstructure, and the Hedgehog projector between the 5-inch gun mounts. The white object near the top of the foremast, below the air-search radar antenna, was the radome for a surface-search radar.

As viewed from the foremast, 5-inch gun mount number 1 was immediately to the rear of the wildcats. Toward the bottom is the flying bridge above the pilothouse, with a searchlight in both forward corners. One level below each searchlight is a 20 mm gun mount and shield.

Despite the visual clutter of the background, details of the upper part of the foremast are visible, including work platforms for the radar antennas and the yardarm, with an IFF (identification friend or foe) ski-pole antenna and a navigating light on the outer end of each side. Also in view are features on the upper level of the superstructure, including the flying bridge and a 20 mm gun mount on each wing.

TANEY IN WORLD WAR II 49

The entire upper level of the superstructure is in view. To the rear of the foremast is the flag bag, in which signal flags were stored. On a round platform with a railing, to the immediate front of the foremast and below the searchlight platform on the foremast, is an optical rangefinder. In a tub just below and forward of the rangefinder is a Mk. 51 director.

From above the smokestack (*bottom center*) facing aft, the 5-inch/38-caliber gun mounts 3 and 4 are in view. Between the smokestack and 5-inch gun mount number 3 are two 20 mm gun mounts, with weather covers over the guns. Between those guns is the mainmast, with the ensign flying from the gaff on the rear of the mast.

In a different view of the aft part of *Taney* at Mare Island in January 1944, aft of the two 20 mm guns just aft of the smokestack, and one level below, are two more 20 mm gun mounts. On the quarterdeck aft of 5-inch gun mount number 3 is a loading machine, a training device for 5-inch gun crews to improve their proficiency in loading the real guns. To the right of 5-inch gun mount 3 is a K-gun, for throwing depth charges to the side of the ship.

Following the completion of her modernization at the Navy Yard, Mare Island, California, *Taney* steamed out into San Francisco Bay, where this series of photos was taken on February 18, 1944, to document her new appearance. The changes to the upper part of the superstructure and the installation of the four new 5-inch/38-caliber gun mounts and the alterations to the superstructure and the deckhouse to accommodate them had profoundly altered the ship's silhouette. *Mare Island Museum*

Taney is viewed from the starboard quarter, 135 degrees off the centerline, with the San Francisco–Oakland Bay Bridge in the background. A life raft standing on its side is lashed to the forward end of the depth-charge rack on the fantail, and more life rafts are secured to the rails along the main deck and on the side of the superstructure. *National Archives*

Taney is viewed from more toward the stern. The bracing supporting the rears of the depth-charge racks is evident. Jutting from the side of the hull is the starboard propeller guard.

Taney lies off Telegraph Hill (*right*), San Francisco, on February 18, 1944. On the port side of the flagstaff on the stern, in an opening in the bulwark, is the smoke generator, with a canvas cover on it. Both of the propeller guards are in view. *National Archives*

Alcatraz Island looms in the left background in a bow-on photo of *Taney* in San Francisco Bay on February 18, 1944. The starboard anchor is secured in the hawsepipe, while the port anchor is dangling below its hawsepipe. The redesigned upper superstructure is visible.

This sequence of photos of *Taney* docked at San Francisco is dated February 18, 1944. Newly installed features are circled, including 5-inch/38-caliber gun mounts 1 and 2, the Hedgehog projector, and the 20 mm gun mounts on the superstructure. The ship had been entirely repainted during her time at the Navy Yard, Mare Island, evidently in the same Measure 12 graded camouflage she had had since the spring of 1942. *Mare Island Museum*

A 20 mm gun mount and 5-inch/38-caliber gun mounts 3 and 4 are circled in this view facing the fantail. Atop the enclosed shield of the number 3 mount is the open hatch door that the mount captain used to observe outside. On the quarterdeck to the right of center is a K-gun, next to which is a storage rack for depth charges. *Mare Island Museum*

Newly mounted 20 mm guns and the 5-inch/38-caliber gun mount number 3 are circled in this image. To the rear of the smokestack, on a raised platform, is the aft rangefinder.

In an undated photo of *Taney* in San Francisco Bay, probably taken around late February 1944, the port anchor has been lowered. The starboard davits, with a boat suspended from them, have been swung out.

This photo of *Taney* taken off her starboard bow evidently was taken on the same occasion as the preceding photo. There is weathering and staining present on the hull that was not present in the February 18, 1944, photos of the ship in San Francisco Bay.

Taney displays her starboard side in San Francisco Bay around late February 1944. This was the only Coast Guard cutter, in Navy service, to be armed with four single 5-inch/38-caliber gun mounts with enclosed shields. These weapons gave *Taney* an appearance somewhat similar to a destroyer.

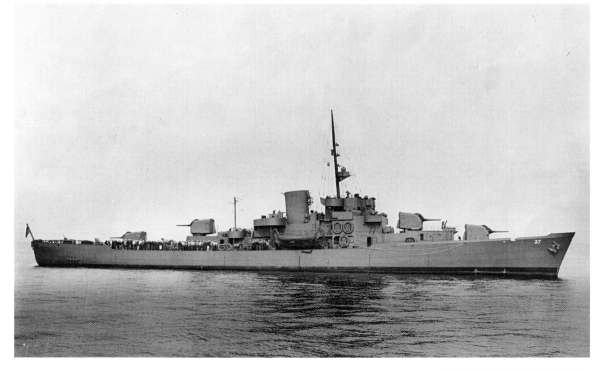

Following her modernization at Mare Island, *Taney* was ordered to the Atlantic, arriving in Boston, Massachusetts, on March 14, 1944. There, a combat information center was installed in the ship. The ship departed Norfolk, Virginia, in early April with Task Force 66, serving as guide ship for convoy UGS-38. This photo and the next two were taken from the forecastle in April. Here, 5-inch/38-caliber gun mounts 1 and 2 are shown with the pieces elevated and trained forward.

Taney's 5-inch gun mounts 1 and 2 are trained partially to starboard. In the foreground are the combined wildcats and capstans.

Both guns are trained to starboard. The crew door on the side of the enclosed shield of gun mount number 1 is open. Water hoses are laid out on the deck.

As seen from the quarterdeck in April 1944, the national ensign waves over 5-inch/38-caliber gun mount number 3. To seal off the space between the gun shields and the gun barrels of the 5-inch mounts, covers known as blast bags, or bucklers, were installed.

The camouflage scheme that *Taney* exhibits in this April 1944 photo is not the same as the one she received at Mare Island earlier that year. It is a graded scheme, as was the one at Mare Island, but now the demarcation between the darker, lower color and the lighter, upper one was below the hawsepipe on the bow, whereas earlier it was above the hawsepipe. The scheme seen here appears to be Measure 22, which is consistent with the period and the dramatic difference in tones between the lower and the upper colors. This camouflage scheme consisted of Navy Blue (5-N) on the hull below the lowest level of the main deck, Haze Gray (5-H) on remaining vertical surfaces, and Deck Blue (20-B) on horizontal surfaces.

Taney is observed nearly broadside from the starboard side, probably on the same occasion as the preceding photo during duty with Convoy UGS-38 in the Atlantic or Mediterranean in April 1944. Several transport vessels are faintly visible in the background.

The crews of the two aft 5-inch/38-caliber guns are conducting firing practice during April 1944. In the foreground is a 20 mm gun with a cover over it; the crewman next to it is standing next to a 20 mm ammunition locker. To the immediate rear of the smokestack is the aft rangefinder.

Taney arrived with Convoy UGS-38 at Bizerte, Tunisia, on April 22, 1944. Two cargo ships and the destroyer USS *Lansdale* (DD-426) had been sunk by German aerial torpedoes during the transit on the night of April 20. A photographer on the ship snapped this photo of wreckage, possibly a dredger, in Bizerte Harbor.

The city of Bizerte forms the backdrop for a photo of the masts and smokestack of a sunken ship in the harbor, in April 1944.

In the foreground is a ship that was destroyed in Bizerte Harbor; moored to the wreckage to the right of it is a small Allied landing craft. In the background is another ship, which appears to have been at least damaged.

A photo from *Taney* of Bizerte shows US Army cargo trucks and cranes parked on the waterfront.

Crewmen of *Taney* take part in a baseball game. In the background is the British cargo ship *Ocean Gallant*, built in Portland, Maine, and transferred to the British under the Lend-Lease Program.

From another angle, *Taney* is visible moored alongside a quay at Bizerte as her crewmen play a game of baseball. Doors on the ship, including on the enclosed gun shields of the 5-inch gun mounts, are open for ventilation.

Several vehicles, including a Dodge WC truck with "U.S. NAVY" and "BIZERTE BUS" painted on the canvas side panel, are dropping off and picking up personnel at the Red Cross Club, formerly a bar and casino. After a sea voyage of several weeks and the tensions of enduring a nighttime aerial attack by Luftwaffe bombers, the crewmen of *Taney* enjoyed their liberty during the week they spent at Bizerte.

A member of *Taney*'s crew photographed the Grand Hotel Continental in Bizerte; this facility likely was used for billeting US naval officers, judging by the officers and shore patrolmen outside the building. *Taney* remained in Bizerte until April 30, 1944. Following the return voyage across the Atlantic, she arrived at the Navy Yard, New York, on May 21, 1944.

Members of the crew of *Taney* visited an airfield at Bizerte, where they viewed this destroyed Focke-Wulf Fw 190 fighter.

As part of Task Force 66, *Taney* escorted another convoy, UGS-45, departing from Norfolk for North Africa on June 11, 1944. In this undated series of photos, *Taney* takes on fuel from the tanker USS *Cossatot* (AO-77) in the Atlantic. The likely date was June 21, since that was the only at-sea refueling recorded in *Taney*'s deck log during that crossing. Here, lines have been rigged from *Taney* (*left*) to *Cossatot* with which to bring a fuel hose from the tanker to *Taney*. In the foreground are two storage racks filled with fin-stabilized depth charges, between which is a K-gun.

A fuel hose has now been strung between *Taney* and *Cossatot*. During the refueling, it was necessary for the two ships to maintain the same course and to keep within a predetermined distance of each other. There was some slack in the fuel hose to allow for some deviation in the distance.

The crewmen in the foreground are manhandling the fuel hose, with the tanker *Cossatot* steaming alongside. In the foreground, to the left are depth charges in a storage rack, while lying on the deck is an arbor-and-cradle assembly. This is attached to a depth charge, and the arbor part is inserted into the K-gun for launching. The arbor and cradle are jettisoned from the depth charge after it is fired. *A. D. Baker III collection*

A photo of the aft part of *Taney* from June 1944 features a 20 mm gun mount and crew in the foreground. The gunner is viewing into a Mk. 14 gunsight. This device, developed by Dr. Charles Draper of the Massachusetts Institute of Technology, had the ability to track the vertical and lateral rates of change of a target's trajectory, calculating the correct aiming point for the gunner. Standing next to the gunner is a talker, who received and transmitted messages through an intercom. His helmet was specially designed to allow the user to wear a headphone set under it.

After serving as a convoy escort from the East Coast of the United States to North Africa with Task Force 66 in 1943, in October of that year *Taney* arrived at the Boston Navy Yard, where she was converted to an amphibious group command (AGC) ship. This involved creating quarters for an embarked flag officer and his staff and installing more communications and radar equipment, resulting in a larger, two-level deckhouse aft of the smokestack. Also, the main battery was altered by replacing the four enclosed 5-inch/38-caliber gun mounts with two single, open, 5-inch/38-caliber gun mounts. Twin 40 mm and single 20 mm gun mounts also were installed. After completion of this conversion in January 1945, *Taney* was transferred to the Pacific theater of operations, where she saw combat in the Okinawa Campaign. This photo, taken in Japan after the end of the war, shows the ship with the October 1944–January 1945 modifications. *Ketenheim collection*

CHAPTER 4
Post–World War II Service

Although the war was over, *Taney*'s duties in the Far East were not. RAdm. Cobb transferred his flag to the battleship *Texas* on August 29, but *Taney* again became a flagship on September 4, when Capt. S. W. King came aboard as port director of Kobe and Osaka.

Taney made for Kobe but was unable to enter because the harbor had not yet been swept for mines. Instead, she made for Wakayama to aid in the evacuation of prisoners of war, anchoring there on September 11.

Taney remained in this anchorage through September 17, when another typhoon was reported 280 miles away. Although the cutter was firmly secured with both anchors, steam was brought up on all of *Taney*'s boilers so that she could bolt at a moment's notice.

Capt. King left the ship on October 13, and the next day, *Taney*, no longer a flagship, steamed toward the US mainland, taking on fuel at Midway. She tied up at Government Island, Alameda.

While invaluable during amphibious landings, the AGC configuration of *Taney* was nearly useless for a Coast Guard cutter; further, the AGC configuration had stability issues, as had been noted in early 1945—a condition wholly unsuitable for the all-weather, anywhere service required of Coast Guard cutters.

In August 1945, plans began to be put into place to return *Taney* and *Duane* to traditional cutter configuration. Accordingly, *Taney* steamed for the East Coast and Charleston Navy Yard, arriving there November 29.

On December 5, 1945, the secretary of the US Navy formally approved the reconversion of the Treasury-class-based AGCs to cutter configuration.

On December 10, 1945, the commandant of the Coast Guard received the following message from the chief of naval operations:

1. The CGC TANEY has been released from duty in the Pacific Fleet and returned to the Coast Guard for operation. Prior to her reporting to the Pacific Fleet the subject cutter was converted for use as an AGC. The Coast Guard now desires that it be restored to its condition prior to being changed to an AGC.

2. It is requested that the CGC TANEY be reconverted as nearly as practicable to its condition as a Coast Guard cutter. As the CGC DUANE is now undergoing a similar reconversion, it is desired that the work be done in accordance with references (a) and (b) which were directives for the CGC DUANE.

3. Attention is invited to reference (c) in which the reconversion of the subject class cutters and authority to expend naval funds for this purpose were approved by the Secretary of the Navy.

Work at Charleston Navy Yard was slow, in part because of a reduction in the shipyard labor force, and also due to a lack of urgency. The day after Christmas 1945, it was announced that the Coast Guard would revert to Treasury Department control in January 1946.

By May 1946, *Taney* was back on the West Coast, assigned to the 12th Coast Guard District, based at Government Island, near Alameda, making headlines for her evacuation of injured sailors.

During the Korean War, *Taney*, as well as the rest of the Coast Guard's fleet, remained under the control of the Treasury Department. *Taney* served as an ocean weather station (a duty she also performed during peacetime) at OWS Nan, Victor, and Sugar, as well as performing plane guard duty off Midway, Guam, and Adak—ultimately two five-month cruises.

It was off Adak on July 2, 1953, that *Taney* was called upon for a search-and-rescue operation after a US Navy PBM Mariner went down due to an engine fire and bad weather. Sadly, of the twelve men aboard, only one body was recovered.

In January 1955, *Taney* began a nine-week cruise of the Pacific named Operation Troll. Water samples were drawn, as well as fish caught and dissected, which scientists aboard tested for signs of radiation that could be attributed to the various nuclear tests that the US government had been conducting in the Pacific.

The remainder of the 1950s and early 1960s could be described as routine but filled with hard work. For a portion of that time, *Taney* served as a training ship.

Portholes in the hull, which had been eliminated during the conversion of *Taney* for USN service, were restored during the 1945–46 reconversion. The cylindrical structure to the rear of the twin 40 mm gun mount contained the Mk. 51 director for that mount. Atop the pilothouse is a new, drum-shaped structure, on top of which is what appears to be a Mk. 52 director, a radar-equipped device for controlling the 5-inch gun. *A. D. Baker III collection*

Following her return to the United States after World War II, *Taney* proceeded to the US Navy Shipyard, Charleston, South Carolina, for conversion back to a US Coast Guard cutter. This work commenced on November 29, 1945. As seen in this sequence of photos taken at Charleston on May 5, 1946, after the conclusion of the conversion, the armaments were restricted to a single 5-inch/38-caliber gun mount with an enclosed shield on the foredeck, with two twin 40 mm gun mounts to the rear of the 5-inch mount and two twin 20 mm guns on the 01 level atop the rear of the deckhouse. *A. D. Baker III collection*

During *Taney*'s 1945–46 reconversion, some of the additions to the superstructure and the deckhouse dating from her conversion to an amphibious group command ship in late 1944 were removed, giving her a less top-heavy appearance. Platforms that previously supported gun mounts had been removed. *A. D. Baker III collection*

On May 1, 1965, *Taney* was redesignated as a high-endurance cutter, or WHEC, a new designation created when the service began to commission the even-larger (378 foot) cutters. In 1966, while en route to Ocean Weather Station November, *Taney*'s starboard prop loosened and dropped to the ocean floor. Despite this, *Taney* completed her thirty-day assignment, then returned to California for repair. On April 1, 1967, *Taney* and the entire Coast Guard were separated from the Treasury Department and instead became subordinate to the US Department of Transportation.

Taney once again saw combat beginning in April 1967, when she was assigned to Coastal Surveillance Force 115. This force coordinated sea, land, and air assets of Operation Market Time, headquartered at Cam Ranh Bay, charged with preventing enemy equipment and materials from reaching South Vietnam by sea. The high-endurance cutters assigned to Market Time were formed into Coast Guard Squadron 3 (RONTHREE) and were on ten-month tours from their home ports.

Taney's average Market Time patrol along the coast of Vietnam was thirty days and involved supporting Swift boats, naval gunfire support, surveillance, interdiction of suspect vessels and medical support for military personnel and the civilian population. Ammunition expenditures during gunfire support operations were such that spent 5-inch brass was stacked on *Taney*'s deck like cordwood.

In January 1970, the starboard propeller shaft broke, reducing *Taney*'s top speed to about 8 knots. Repair ship USS *Tuttila* removed the prop and broken shaft, which were secured to *Taney*'s fantail. The cutter then limped to Subic Bay for permanent repair. By the time the repairs were complete, *Taney*'s deployment was over, and she steamed for San Francisco by way of Guam and Hawaii, encountering a typhoon along the way. Although she took on water, the veteran cutter weathered the storm.

Taney arrived at San Francisco on March 3, 1970. During her time in Vietnamese waters, she fired 3,345 rounds—95 tons—at the enemy, treated 6,000 Vietnamese civilians, and inspected 1,000 vessels.

Taney lingered in California only briefly, since she was assigned the new duty station of Norfolk, Virginia. She steamed from Alamdea for the last time on February 8, 1971. *Taney* arrived in Norfolk on March 10, staying only briefly before putting into the Curtis Bay Coast Guard Yard near Baltimore for overhaul, rehabilitation, and modernization, a process that was completed in July 1972.

The work equipped the venerable *Taney* with a modern air-conditioning system, better heads with retention toilets, larger berths and improved communications, an overhaul of her machinery, and notably a new weather search radar in a bulbous dome above the bridge.

That radar as *Taney*[[AU: ???]] became the prime ship manning Ocean Weather Station Hotel, 200 miles off Delaware, where the warm Gulf Stream and cool air off the mainland met. The station was normally operated from August 1 through April 15. *Taney* went on station seven times yearly, conducting twenty-one deployments until sophisticated land-based radar, satellites, and buoys finally made Hotel, the last OWS, obsolete, and the operation ceased on September 30, 1977.

It was from OWS Hotel that during a severe storm in 1976, *Taney*'s men rescued the crew of a distressed shrimp boat—earning the ship and her crew a meritorious unit citation.

Relieved of weather duties, *Taney* resumed the operations for which she was originally built—search and rescue and interdiction of smugglers. In January 1978, *Taney* intercepted the *Misioty*, which had 8 tons of marijuana aboard, which at the time had an estimated street value of $10 million. This was topped in September of the next year, when *Taney*'s men boarded the shrimper *San Jose* and found an estimated 14 tons of marijuana in her holds.

These paled in comparison to a seizure late in *Taney*'s career, 300 miles east of Cape Hatteras. This operation was reported in the October 4, 1985, *Washington Times* as follows:

Jacksonville, FL: The CG cutter *Taney* returned to port . . . after seizing an estimated 160 tons of marijuana, the largest such bust on record.

The 4,176 bales of marijuana that were seized have an estimated street value of $132 million, Coast Guard officials said. "That's what we're here to do," said Cmdr. Robert Hoyt, the *Taney*'s skipper, after the ship docked in the St. John's River. He said crew members would paint another marijuana leaf on the ship's tower to mark the latest bust; 10 leaves are there already.

The *Taney* . . . followed the *Sea Maid I* and its 175-foot barge for more than 1½ days, Hoyt said. The tug and its barge were "loitering" about 300 miles east of Cape Hatteras when the arrests were made. . . . The vessels had been staying in an area about 50 miles square, apparently waiting to make contact with smaller boats that would take the marijuana ashore. When that didn't happen, the Coast Guard made contact.

For security reasons, the arrests were not reported until last weekend. Although the *Taney*'s homeport [*sic*] is Portsmouth, Virginia, the seized vessels were brought here because it is the nearest port where the Vice President's Joint Task Force Group has an office.

Two pairs of davits and three boats are on the starboard side of the deckhouse. Aft of the smokestack, most of the second level of the superstructure had been removed during the recent reconversion, except for the part just aft of the smokestack. The height of this section was increased, and a large bay door was on its rear. *A. D. Baker III collection*

In a May 5, 1946, aerial view off *Taney*'s starboard bow, the newly installed 5-inch/38-caliber enclosed gun mount, the twin 40 mm gun mount, and the gun-director tower to the rear of the 40 mm mount are in view. The searchlight platform on the foremast, which was moved down to the level of the top of the smokestack during the October 1944 to January 1945 modifications, was now above the level of the top of the smokestack. *A. D. Baker III collection*

Asked where the *Sea Maid* was headed, Cdr. Hoyt replied, "I think that she was where she was supposed to be. We're getting more and more mother ship operations up toward the north."

A spokesman for the Drug Enforcement Administration said it was the largest seizure in US history. . . . The *Sea Maid* was flying the Honduran flag, but was seized as a stateless vessel after the Honduran government refuted the claim of registry, the Coast Guard said.

Not quite a year later, in September 1986, the decision was made that the time had come for *Taney* to be decommissioned. The date selected was December 7, 1986, the forty-fifth anniversary of her action in Hawaii—an action that by this time she was the sole surviving combat ship of.

Her final commanding officer, Cmdr. Winston G. Churchill, as well as her crew, were keenly aware that *Taney*'s future service would be that of a museum ship, memorializing the efforts of the men who had built her fifty years past, the twenty-eight captains who had commanded her, and the thousands of coast guardsmen who proudly declared themselves *Taney* crewmen at war and peace.

Great care was taken to leave the ship appearing as if she were ready to steam out of port on another patrol. The decommissioning ceremony at Coast Guard Support Center Portsmouth was carefully planned. At the beginning of the ceremony, Marjorie Coffin, widow of RAdm. Coffin, *Taney*'s first commanding officer, presented Cmdr. Churchill with a red carnation lei. As her crew manned the rails, various dignitaries made speeches. After the National Anthem was played, the executive officer reported to Churchill, "Sir, the Coast Guard Cutter *Taney* is prepared for decommissioning."

Cmdr. Churchill then repeated to the reviewing admiral that "Coast Guard Cutter *Taney* is prepared for decommissioning," who replied, "Very well, sir; carry out the decommissioning.

One by one, *Taney*'s crew presented themselves to the officer of the deck, saluted, turned, saluted the colors, and marched off the ship, until there was only one. Then Cmdr. Churchill turned to the colors, saluted the colors, and left the ship.

The colors were lowered, ending decades of service to the people of the United States. That flag was folded and fittingly presented to one more dignitary present, Corinne Taney Marks, the seventy-two-year old lady who had christened the ship as its sponsor fifty years, one month, and thirteen days earlier.

Several noteworthy features are in this May 5, 1946, photograph. Above the deck is a rolled-up sun tarpaulin. Two twin 20 mm gun mounts are side by side on the 01 level at the rear of the deckhouse. Rearward-slanting flying bridges project from the 01 level of the deckhouse. The second level of the deckhouse served as a storage bay: visible inside is the front of a jeep. *A. D. Baker III collection*

Taney is steaming off from the Navy Yard, Charleston, South Carolina, in early May 1946. The ship's name is painted in small, dark letters on the stern. The ship was painted in a light color, but evidently not white, as is evident when comparing that color to the white paint on the boat under the rear davits and on the inside of the bay door of the second level of the deckhouse. *A. D. Baker III collection*

After being converted back to USCG standards, *Taney* returned to the Pacific. For the rest of the 1940s, the cutter often was engaged in weather patrols in the Pacific, gathering data to allow meteorologists from the National Weather Service to forecast weather conditions along the world's major air and sea routes. Here, the ship is viewed from the fantail as she lists to starboard in rough waters during a weather patrol. *Ketenheim collection*

Taney is along a dock at the US Coast Guard base at Government Island (since renamed Coast Guard Island), Alameda, California, during 1951. On the bow are draft marks: numbers that indicate the distance from the bottom of the keel to the waterline of the ship. On the hull above the waterline is a black stripe called the boot topping. Its purpose is to mask the oil and other pollutants that cling to the ship in any busy harbor. *Ketenheim collection*

During 1951, *Taney* is underway off the California coast. In the summer of the previous year, the Korean War erupted. In this war, the Coast Guard maintained custody of this cutter, and during the conflict she was rearmed for antisubmarine warfare. However, *Taney* spent the war mostly engaged in weather patrols and air-sea rescue as far north as Alaska. Painted on the bow is "W37." By the time this photo was taken, a Hedgehog projector had been installed to the front of the pilothouse. *Ketenheim collection*

As part of *Taney*'s search-and-rescue mission, on July 2, 1953, the crew of the cutter performed a search for survivors of a Martin PBM Mariner that disappeared over the Pacific off Adak, Alaska. During a search of the crash scene, *Taney* recovered one body; the entire complement of the aircraft perished. This wreckage on the deck of *Taney* was all that was salvaged of the Mariner. Near the edge of the deck are depth-charge ready racks and K-guns.

Taney slices through the water off a coastline on October 27, 1955. A close examination of this photo and the preceding aerial view of the ship in 1951 disclose that at least one mine rack had been installed on the fantail sometime between 1946 and 1951. *A. D. Baker III collection*

Sometime during 1955, *Taney* is moored to Pier 9, Honolulu, Hawaii Territory. All the various guns are painted in a dark shade. *Taney* visited Honolulu that year during her service with a scientific survey of the effects of nuclear testing on the populations and nature in the Pacific. This voyage took the cutter from San Francisco across the ocean as far as Tokyo. *Ketenheim collection*

In a dramatic photo illustrating the effects of rough seas on a smaller ship such as a USCG cutter, *Taney* bucks waves at high speed, racing to the scene of a ship, SS *Angelo Petri*, in distress, on February 9, 1960. The hull is visible to the keel as the bow rises out of the water. *Taney* assisted in the rescue of the crew of the *Petri* after that ship took on a large volume of water, shorting out the main switchboard and rendering the vessel out of control in the Pacific off the entrance to San Francisco Bay. *Ketenheim collection*

During an official visit to the United States in late April 1960, President Charles de Gaulle of France is greeted by officers of *Taney*, including the ship's commanding officer, Frank V. Helmer (*to the left*). Subsequently, DeGaulle was treated to a tour of San Francisco Bay on *Taney*. *Ketenheim collection*

This August 1963 photo is one of the last ones of *Taney* before the old mainmast was taken down and replaced by a tripod mast. The photo was taken in the Pacific off San Francisco. The davits supporting the forward whaleboat have been swung out, so the boat is casting its shadow on the side of the hull of the cutter. *A. D. Baker III collection*

Several changes are visible in this July 6, 1964, photo of *Taney* underway in San Francisco Bay. The mainmast has been replaced by a tripod mast, to support the big air-search radar antenna. A second level has been built atop the aft part of the deckhouse, and the two twin 20 mm gun mounts have been removed from the 01 level on the very rear of the deckhouse. Two large whip antennas have been mounted atop the pilothouse. An "E" representing an award for Excellence has been marked on the smokestack. *A. D. Baker III collection*

In May 1966, *Taney* is closely shadowing the Soviet freighter *Chernjakhovsk* in international waters off the coast of Northern California. The cutter was tasked with keeping watch on the Soviet ship because the Russians were employing commercial vessels to monitor US military radio traffic. At the top is a wing float of the flying boat from which the photograph was taken. In the interim since the preceding photo from July 6, 1966, had been taken, the twin 40 mm gun mount, its "tub" splinter shield, and the tower behind it for the director had been removed from the 01 level at the front of the superstructure. *Ketenheim collection*

While based at Alameda, California, *Taney* departs on a patrol in July 1968. The cutter had recently been given high-visibility markings on the sides of the hull: two diagonal stripes, with the US Coast Guard insignia on the wider stripe, and the inscription "COAST GUARD." *A. D. Baker III collection*

During the Vietnam War, US Coast Guard high-endurance cutters based on the West Coast took turns deploying to Vietnam for tours of duty. *Taney* was assigned to a ten-month tour in the war zone from April 1969 to February 1970 as part of Operation Market Time, a joint US–South Vietnamese maritime effort to interdict supplies destined to the enemy by sea. Here, troops from the US 173rd Airborne Brigade are on the fantail of *Taney* as the cutter transports them to a landing site in the Mekong delta, in August 1969. During this mission, *Taney* also would provide fire support for these troops. *Ketenheim collection*

Taney's August 1969 sortie into enemy-held territory with the 173rd Airborne Brigade entailed rooting out enemy forces in encampments, bunkers, and tunnels. The troopers in this photo, on the deck of the cutter, have brought with them a German shepherd war dog, who will help them sniff out enemy combatants. *Ketenheim collection*

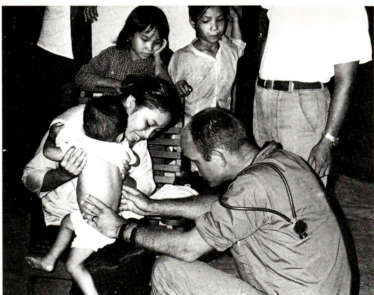

While on deployment to the Republic of Vietnam, the medical personnel of *Taney* occasionally performed medical services for the local civilian populace, under the Medical Civilian Assistance Program (MEDCAP). Hospital Corpsman 1st Class Ken "Doc" Fincher, from *Taney*, is examining a toddler during one such MEDCAP mission. *Ketenheim collection*

During her deployment to Southeast Asia in 1969, *Taney* visits Hong Kong. In addition to the US Coast Guard insignia on the diagonal stripe on the hull, the insignia also was applied to the smokestack. The cutter's number, 37, is on the bow and on the stern. *Ketenheim collection*

In early March 1970, *Taney* returned to San Francisco Bay, California, following her ten-month-long rotation to Vietnam. She is cruising past the San Francisco–Oakland Bay Bridge, en route to her base at Coast Guard Island, Alameda, California, where family members will greet the crew members upon their return. Flying from the masts is a 160-foot-long streamer, in honor of her 160-man crew. *Ketenheim collection*

Around 1971, the crew of *Taney* enjoys a cookout on the quarterdeck. Morale-improving events such as this were called "steel beach" parties, since they replicated a beach party, only on the deck of a ship. The older man with a short-sleeved white shirt standing in line toward the left is a National Weather Service employee, part of the ship's weather-data-collecting personnel. Relaxed grooming standards in effect in the Coast Guard at the time are in evidence in the form of longer hair, sideburns, and facial hair. *Ketenheim collection*

Crewmen on the fantail of *Taney* are hauling on a line during a towing exercise at Ocean Weather Station Victor, in the Pacific, around 1971. This was to maintain their proficiency in towing other vessels, a task sometimes conducted by USCG cutters. In the background is USCG cutter *Wachusett* (WHEC-44), an Owasco-class high-endurance cutter. Details of the bracing for the bulwark along the fantail are in view. *Ketenheim collection*

In February 1972, *Taney* proceeded to her new base at Norfolk, Virginia. Shortly after her arrival, she proceeded to the Curtis Bay Coast Guard Yard in Maryland for a rehabilitation and modernization (RAM) refitting. Part of the modifications was a spherical storm-search radome, erected atop the pilothouse. After the overhaul, *Taney* commenced weather-station duties in the Atlantic. The new storm-search radome is evident in this view of the cutter on duty at Ocean Station "Hotel" on August 8, 1973. The Hedgehog projector had been removed from the 02 level to the front of the pilothouse. *A. D. Baker III collection*

When *Taney* was docked at the USCG station at Portsmouth, Virginia, near the end of 1973, a smiley face had been temporarily painted on the storm-search radome. The hull exhibits a stained and weather-beaten appearance: evidence of her recent service on the weather station in the stormy Atlantic. *Ketenheim collection*

For four years (1973–77), *Taney* was assigned to patrolling Ocean Station "Hotel," a weather-monitoring zone some 200 miles off the East Coast. The cutter is seen in this aerial view during one of those patrols. Two loop antennas on masts are on the quarterdeck, and these are visible in earlier photos of the ship. *Ketenheim collection*

Taney is entering Chesapeake Bay following her last patrol on Ocean Station "Hotel," on September 30, 1977. The cutter had regularly patrolled that station since 1973. However, weather-tracking technology was advancing rapidly, and *Taney* was being replaced at "Hotel" by a weather-data-gathering buoy. *A. D. Baker III collection*

After being retired from weather-station duty in the Atlantic, the storm-tracking radome was removed from above the pilothouse of *Taney*. This is evident in a view of the cutter during a visit to Toulon, France, while deployed to the Mediterranean on June 13, 1981. Since the late 1970s, the large air-search radar antenna had been absent from the tripod mainmast. Also, sometime after September 1977, the large opening on each side of the superstructure had been plated over. *A. D. Baker III collection*

Taney is viewed from the starboard quarter while underway in Toulon Harbor on June 13, 1981. On the side of the superstructure, one level below the navigating bridge and the pilothouse, is an "E" award letter, with three hash marks below it. A close examination reveals that the "E" award with three hash marks also is present on the smokestack below the USCG insignia, adjacent to which is marked "DC" with one hash mark below it. The dark area on the side of the navigating bridge is a display of the ship's campaign and award ribbons. *A. D. Baker III collection*

CHAPTER 5
Museum Ship

Taney was donated to the City of Baltimore, which had the cutter towed first to Bethlehem Key Highway Shipyard for storage. While there, she was declared a National Historic Landmark on January 27, 1988, before finally being towed to Baltimore's Inner Harbor, where she opened as a museum in 1989.

After fifty years of active service, the USCG cutter *Taney* was decommissioned at Portsmouth, Virginia, on December 7, 1986: exactly forty-five years after the ship saw action in the defense of Pearl Harbor from the Japanese attack on December 7, 1941. *Taney* was the last surviving warship present in that attack. Members of the crew stand at attention on the pier as the final commanding officer of *Taney*, Cmdr. Winston G. Churchill, walks down the gangway. The names of the cutter and her commanding officer are on the windscreen on the gangway. Present at the decommissioning were the ship's sponsor, Mrs. Corinne Taney Marks, and Marjorie B. Coffin, the widow of the ship's first commanding officer, Cmdr. E. A. Coffin. *Ketenheim collection*

Taney left her berth at the Baltimore Maritime Museum in mid-March 2003 and proceeded to a drydock at the US Coast Guard Yard, Curtis Bay, Maryland, where she received an overhaul. This series of photographs was taken by Jet Lowe upon the cutter's arrival at the drydock on March 14. Here *Taney* is afloat in the drydock, as viewed from off the port stern. *Library of Congress*

Taney is viewed from a lower angle upon her arrival in the drydock at Curtis Bay. This was the first major maintenance work performed on the ship since October 2001, when twenty-eight 6" × 12" zinc anodes were temporarily affixed to the hull below the waterline to provide cathodic protection against corrosion.

Once the cutter had been carefully positioned in the drydock exactly above a series of wooden blocks that would support the ship, a gigantic Synrcolift on the bottom of the drydock lifted *Taney* clear of the water. Before the lifting process, the hull was painstakingly positioned over a gigantic carriage on the platform, which would bear the full weight of the ship while it was out of the water. *Library of Congress*

Taney is viewed from forward of the starboard bow. The ship is resting on a blocking carriage, which has trucks, or wheels, that are positioned on steel tracks that are flush with the surface of the lift platform. This allowed the ship to be placed in its final position on the platform. Wooden blocks are between the top of the carriage and the bottom of the hull. *Library of Congress*

Taney is seen from directly ahead of her bow. Drydocked to her port side is USCGC *Maria Bray* (WLM-562). The initial inspection of the hull revealed that some marine growth was present, along with isolated areas of severe corrosion and pitting. *Library of Congress*

Draft marks, to indicate the distance of the actual waterline from the level of the keel, are above and aft of the starboard propeller. Scaffolding for workers has been moved alongside the hull, adjacent to the bilge keel. *Library of Congress*

MUSEUM SHIP 95

In a view off the starboard stern, one of the two loop antennas on the quarterdeck of *Taney* is visible to the right of the tripod mainmast. The rudder and the starboard propeller and propeller shaft are in the foreground. Farther forward, on the lower part of the hull, is the starboard bilge keel, a long, curved, finlike structure designed to reduce the roll of the ship. *Library of Congress*

Corrosion and marine growth formed rough areas on the propellers, propeller shafts, shaft struts, and hull. The underwater part of the hull was cleaned and stripped down to bare metal with 40,000 psi hydroblasting, taking about eleven days to achieve. Holes and defects in the hull were repaired by welding steel patches, and also by applying a durable, two-part repair composite material. During the 2003 overhaul, both of the ship's 3,400-pound bronze propellers were permanently removed, to lower the chance of corrosion forming on the stern due to the proximity of the dissimilar metal of the propellers. *Library of Congress*

A photo of the starboard stern and propeller facing aft also includes the skeg, along the centerline of the bottom of the hull and terminating forward of the rudder. Blocks are between the bottom of the skeg and the platform. Toward the right are two poppets, which help bear the weight of the outer part of the hull. *Library of Congress*

The blocking carriage that supports *Taney* in drydock is seen from near the starboard bow of the cutter at the time of the ship's arrival at the Coast Guard Yard at Curtis Bay, Maryland. The wooden blocks between the carriage and the hull were carefully positioned below the ship's frames, to avoid damaging the shell plates of the hull. Once the hull was cleaned and repaired, it was coated with Ameron 385 epoxy paint, with glass-flake additive to improve coating durability. The overhaul was completed in April 2003, and the cutter was towed back to the Baltimore Maritime Museum. *Library of Congress*

The following series of photographs documents features of the USCG cutter *Taney* as displayed at Historic Ships in Baltimore. This museum combines the former Baltimore Maritime Museum and the USS *Constellation* Museum in the Inner Harbor of Baltimore, Maryland. *Author*

In a view off the bow, *Taney* displays her overall Coast Guard White paint scheme. The boot topping on the hull above and below the waterline is black. The masts and boat davits are painted in a tan color. Blue covers are on the searchlights and the rails on the flying bridge above the pilothouse. *Author*

MUSEUM SHIP 99

As seen in a view of the starboard bow, the hull was constructed of steel plates, arranged in horizontal rows called strakes. The bottom of each strake overlapped the top of the one below, creating a horizontal shadow along the bottom of each strake. Below each of the hawsepipes, the eye-like protrusions that the shanks of the anchors are housed in, is a steel plate, applied over the strakes to strengthen the hull in this area. This feature is faintly visible here. *Rich Kolasa*

Details of the forward starboard part of the hull are displayed. Draft marks are painted on the bow: white on the boot topping and black above the boot topping. The cutter's number, "37," is in black; the US Coast Guard insignia is on a diagonal red stripe, while a thin blue stripe is to the immediate rear of the red stripe. *Department of Defense*

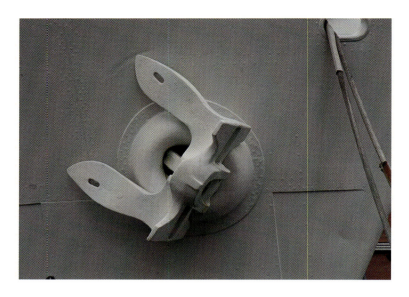

The starboard anchor is observed close-up, the shank of which is nestled in the hawsehole. The upper part of the aforementioned vertical steel plate below the hawsehole is visible. The point of the upper fluke of the anchor has worn a shallow, curved groove into the hull plate behind it. *Author*

Originally *Taney* had numerous portholes on the sides of the hull. These were eliminated and plated over in early 1942, as a damage-control measure, while the cutter was under operational control of the US Navy. Round weld beads are visible in this photograph where portholes were covered with steel plates in 1942. *Rich Kolasa*

In a close-up of the USCG insignia on the starboard side of *Taney*'s hull, to the left is a welded-in patch, and to the right is a recessed fitting, one of many on the hull, for attaching lines to support staging planks for workers to stand on while performing repairs and maintenance on the hull in drydock. *Author*

The single, enclosed 5-inch/38-caliber gun mount with its steel shield is viewed from the starboard side. This weapon is called a mount, not a turret. The enclosure gave the gun crew protection from the elements and from shrapnel and splinters. On the front of the shield are windows with hinged covers for the trainer and the pointer to sight through when the gun was under the control of the crew instead of the director via the fire-control system. On the side of the shield is a crew door. *Rich Kolasa*

In a view from alongside the starboard bow, details of the front of the superstructure and the foremast are visible. Two tall, black whip antennas are mounted on the 01 level atop the forward deckhouse. *Rich Kolasa*

The upper part of the shield of the 5-inch/38-caliber gun mount is visible from the starboard side of the cutter. The cylinder on the upper rear of the shield is part of a mechanism to assist with opening the mount captain's hatch on the roof of the shield. *Author*

The shell, or hull plates, took a beating over the years from ocean waves to bumps with docks or vessels. Many of these are visible on the starboard side of the bow and forward hull. Some of the plugged portholes are in view. *Rich Kolasa*

From the starboard side are seen the first two levels of the forward part of the superstructure (*left*) and the forward deckhouse (*right*). At the upper center is the base of the starboard whip antenna. The portholes have curved gutters above them. *Rich Kolasa*

A large dent is visible on the hull below the letter "T." To the upper left is a locker containing a life raft and survival gear. *Rich Kolasa*

The navigating bridge, the pilothouse, and the structure on the flying bridge above the pilothouse are viewed from the starboard side of the bow. Attached to the top of the bulwark at the front of the navigating bridge is a windscreen, a device that directed oncoming wind upward, giving the personnel on the bridge some protection from the elements. *Rich Kolasa*

The foremast, as seen from the wharf off the starboard side of the superstructure, is equipped with radar antennas, sensors, communications antennas, lights, and a loudspeaker. Toward the bottom is the starboard bridge wing, to the side of the pilothouse; the ship's awards and campaign ribbons are on the bulwark of the wing.

The ribbons representing awards and campaigns on the starboard bridge wing include those for the ship's service in World War II (Victory Medal) and the Korean and Vietnam Wars. Also present are several unit commendations. To the left of the ribbons is a scoreboard of the cutter's interdictions of illegal drug smugglers at sea, represented by marijuana leaves with red *X*s over them. *Author*

The starboard side of the superstructure is observed from the rear. On the side of the main-deck level of the superstructure, a rectangular plate with rounded upper corners is discernible. This was welded over an opening in the superstructure sometime between September 1977 and June 1981, and the same was done on the port side of the superstructure. *Rich Kolasa*

Taney's number 1 motor surfboat is in its chocks on the starboard side of the main deck amidships. The cutter's boats were used for general utility work and rescue operations. The tackle from the davits to the boat is present. The blue bags below the beam between the tops of the davits are for storing the lifelines: knotted ropes for the boat's occupants to climb onto in the event the boat should experience a mishap. Mounted on the deck aft of the forward davit is the operating motor. *Rich Kolasa*

Aft of the bridge is the flag bag, with a blue tarpaulin over it. The flag bag was where the ship's various flags were stored. On the smokestack is the US Coast Guard insignia and a red "E" award for effectiveness in engineering and survivability, below which are three hash marks, representing three additional, consecutive "E" awards. *Rich Kolasa*

The smokestack, surfboat and davits, mainmast, and superstructure are observed from amidships on the starboard side. A number of portholes are on the hull, aft of the USCG insignia. These extend aft, on both sides of the hull, to above the propeller guards. *Rich Kolasa*

MUSEUM SHIP 109

The motor surfboat rests on four heavily cushioned chocks, two per side. Immediately aft of the aft davit is the control stand for the davits. Three safety cables stretch between the davits. *Author*

The amidships area is seen from the starboard side of the cutter. Most of the deckhouse, which stretches aft of the superstructure, is in view; it has second levels forward, below the smokestack, and aft. The lower part of the tripod mainmast is to the left. *Rich Kolasa*

Three acetylene bottles, for welding purposes, are stored in brackets alongside the central part of the deckhouse on the starboard side. A hawser is secured around mooring bitts and is routed out through an open chock. *Rich Kolasa*

Three gasoline drums are stowed on a rack on the starboard side of the main deck alongside the deckhouse. They contained fuel for the motor surfboats. In the event of a fire on the ship, the crew could jettison the drums by releasing the strap. *Author*

MUSEUM SHIP 111

A flying bridge is at the 01 level on each side of the aft part of the deckhouse. Together, these flying bridges gave personnel a virtually unimpeded 360-degree view of the water around the cutter. *Rich Kolasa*

The tripod mainmast is viewed from its starboard quarter. At the apex of the tripod is a platform with a rail around it and yardarms extending from it, above which is a pole mast with ladder rungs on the sides. Rungs also are on the forward leg of the tripod. In the foreground to the left is a loop antenna. *Rich Kolasa*

The mainmast, as observed from starboard, is similar in appearance and appointments to its condition while still in service in the 1980s. One detail that is no longer present is the gaff, on the rear of the platform at the apex of the tripod, from which the ensign (the national flag) was flown when the cutter was at sea. *Rich Kolasa*

Taney is seen from aft. An awning is rigged over the fantail. The flagstaff on the stern is of wooden construction. Below the flagstaff is the stern hawsehole, through which mooring lines are routed. *Author*

Taney is seen from her port quarter. Since the ship now is not laden with the stores, provisions, munitions, and crew normally carried during her operational career, the cutter stands high in the water, with all or most of her boot topping in view above the water. *Rich Kolasa*

A photo of the port aft part of the cutter shows the two loop antennas (*left*), the port propeller guard (*center*), and several portholes. A number of welded patches are discernible on the hull. Above the boot topping, several water discharge ports have been plugged with round plates welded in. Hawseholes are in the gunwales on each side and aft of the flagstaff. *Rich Kolasa*

One of *Taney*'s propellers is displayed on the wharf next to the cutter. Both propellers were removed from the ship during her overhaul in 2003, as a measure to lessen corrosion on the adjacent areas of the hull due to the galvanic effect of two dissimilar metals—bronze and steel—in proximity. *Rich Kolasa*

The port side of *Taney* is in view, from the quarterdeck to the bow. A pontoon boat with two outboard motors is in the chocks below the davits. At some point between 1981 and 1986, the top level of the deckhouse immediately aft of the smokestack was removed, and what remained of that deckhouse on the 01 level was reduced in size, with its rear portion being removed. *Rich Kolasa*

The aft end of the deckhouse and the truncated second level of the deckhouse are viewed from the port side. Also in view is the lower part of the tripod of the mainmast. A chrome-plated ship's bell is on the rear of the deckhouse. *Rich Kolasa*

The deckhouse, smokestack, and superstructure are observed from the wharf to the port side of the quarterdeck. Toward the right is the port loop antenna, with a red base. *Rich Kolasa*

An amidships view of the port side of the cutter discloses the locations of portholes, ladders, rails, ventilators, and other features. On the side of the smokestack is the USCG insignia and the red "E" award with three hash marks below it. *Rich Kolasa*

The port sides of the superstructure and smokestack and forward part of the deckhouse are viewed from a closer perspective. "COAST GUARD" is marked in large letters on the side of the pontoon motorboat. *Rich Kolasa*

Below the port davits, in this overhead view, is the pontoon motorboat. On the inboard sides of the gray pontoons are numerous grab handles. The starboard outboard motor is discernible, clamped to the transom of the boat. *Rich Kolasa*

The pontoon motorboat on the port side of the main deck is viewed from the front. The orange instrument stand and the top of the steering wheel are visible. *Rich Kolasa*

MUSEUM SHIP 121

The superstructure and the forward deckhouse, attached to the front of the superstructure on the main deck, are observed from the port side. When the photo was taken, there was considerable corrosion on the port side of these structures. On the bulwark of the bridge wing are the badly deteriorated remnants of the service ribbons and the drug-bust scorecard. *Rich Kolasa*

The forward half of *Taney* is viewed from the port beam. The gray structure to the side of the 5-inch/38-caliber gun mount is a viewing platform, to allow tourists to view the interior of the gun mount. *Rich Kolasa*

Members from Coast Guard Sector Maryland-National Capital Region and audience members await the start of the Pearl Harbor Remembrance ceremony on former Coast Guard cutter *Taney* in Baltimore Wednesday, December 7, 2016. The event marked the 75th anniversary of the attack on Pearl Harbor. *US Coast Guard photo by Petty Officer 3rd Class Jasmine Mieszala*

On the forecastle are the two combination wildcats/capstans. The wildcats are horizontal wheels that are geared so that the anchor chains fit in them; the windlasses, belowdecks, drove the wildcats, to raise the anchors. The tan drums atop the wildcats are capstans, around which hawsers could be secured to perform mooring and other tasks. To the immediate rear of each wildcat are the controllers and the brake handwheels for the anchor chains. *Rich Kolasa*

The wildcats/capstans, controllers, and brake wheels are seen from the starboard side of the forecastle. The anchor chains pass into the riding chocks, also called the fairleads, from which the chains are routed down through the hawseholes. On the upper parts of the riding chocks are riding pawls, which act as ratchets to prevent the anchor chain from slipping while being raised. To the front of the right wildcat is the chock through which the anchor chain passes down into the chain locker. *Rich Kolasa*

The crew of the single 5-inch/38-caliber gun mount was protected from the elements and from splinters during a firefight by an enclosure called the shield. This gun was a dual-purpose one, meaning that it was effective against aircraft as well as surface targets. *Rich Kolasa*

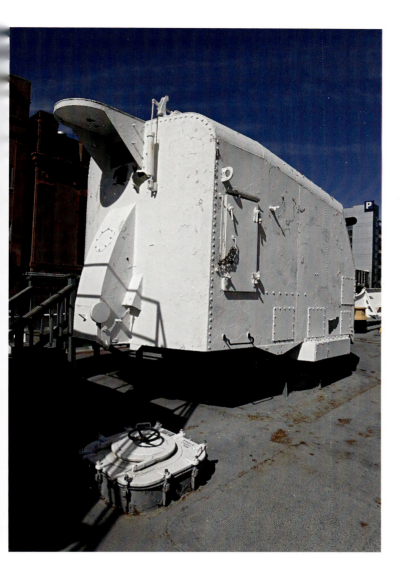 

The shield of the 5-inch/38-caliber gun mount is seen from the right rear. On the side is an entry door for the gun crew, with a black ladder rung below it. The curved platform on the upper rear of the shield was installed in the early 1970s, and it supported an antenna. *Rich Kolasa*

The interior of the rear of the enclosure of the 5-inch/38-caliber gun mount is seen through the left crew door. Up to eleven crewmen had to operate within the close confines of the mount. To the left is the rear of the gun. On the rear bulkhead above the fire extinguisher is a folding platform for the mount captain to stand on when he needed to use his overhead hatch for observation. *Rich Kolasa*

A powder cartridge and shell are seated in the loading tray of the 5-inch/38-caliber gun, to the rear of the breech. The gun was equipped with a powered rammer, for seating the ammunition in the breech. The structure aft of the breech with the data plates on the side is the slide assembly. To the left of center is the ammunition hoist, with a blue training shell in it. *Rich Kolasa*

The space in the left side of the gun mount is displayed. To the front of the ammunition hoist were the pointer's and the fuse setter's stations. Crew helmets are stored under the ceiling. Ready-service projectiles are secured in brackets to the left. Angle irons that form the frame of the roof are at the top. *Rich Kolasa*

The motor surfboat stored on the starboard side of the main deck is observed from the rear. The control stand for the davits is the object with the blue cover over its top, next to the closest davit. Also adjacent to the davit is a capstan. *Rich Kolasa*

MUSEUM SHIP

Three acetylene bottles, for welding purposes, are stored in brackets on the starboard side of the deckhouse. To the upper left is the base of the mainmast. *Rich Kolasa*

Continuing aft on the starboard main deck alongside the aft part of the deckhouse is the rack for three 55-gallon gasoline drums, which provided fuel for the motor surfboat. Above the drums is the starboard flying bridge. This and its counterpart on the port side were installed just after World War II. *Rich Kolasa*

On the quarterdeck aft of the mainmast and the deckhouse are the towing bitt (*left*), for securing a hawser from a ship to be towed, and a capstan (*right*), for pulling other ships or heavy objects. *Rich Kolasa*

MUSEUM SHIP 129

A chrome-plated ship's bell hangs from the rear of the first level of the deckhouse. *Rich Kolasa*

The towing bitt (*left*) and the capstan (*right*) are viewed close-up. The towing bitt is a heavy-duty casting, designed to stand up to the mass of another ship under tow. *Rich Kolasa*

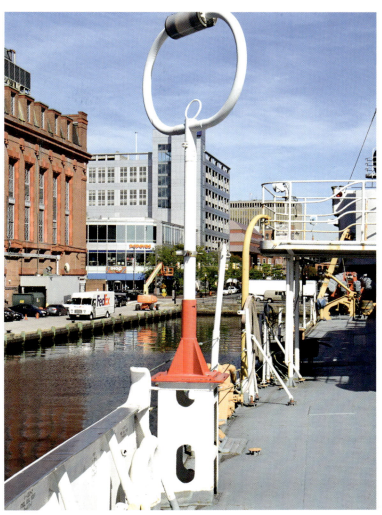

The loop antenna on the port side of the quarterdeck is viewed from the rear. Its mast is mounted on a box-shaped bracket with lightening holes. *Rich Kolasa*

The towing bitt is seen from its forward-port quarter, showing the two horizontal bitts the towing hawser would be wrapped around. The notch at the top of the towing bitt was where the towing hawser would be routed out to the rear. *Rich Kolasa*

The aft part of the main deck is called the fantail. Seen here are several hatches, vents, and the flagstaff. *Rich Kolasa*

The ensign flies from the flagstaff on the stern of *Taney*. This was the authorized location of the national flag when the ship was in port. At sea, the ensign flew from the gaff on the mainmast. *Rich Kolasa*

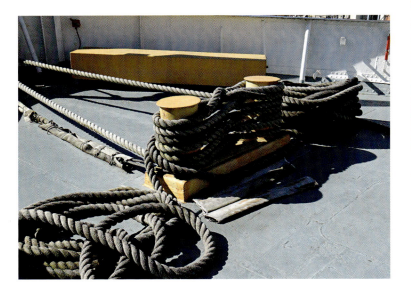

This mooring bitt is on the fantail, near the flagstaff (*out of the view to the left*). In the background is the bulwark on the port side of the deck. *Rich Kolasa*

This passageway on the second deck is part of "officers' country," the part of the ship reserved for officers' staterooms, showers and heads, and wardroom. In the background is a ladder to the quarterdeck. *Rich Kolasa*

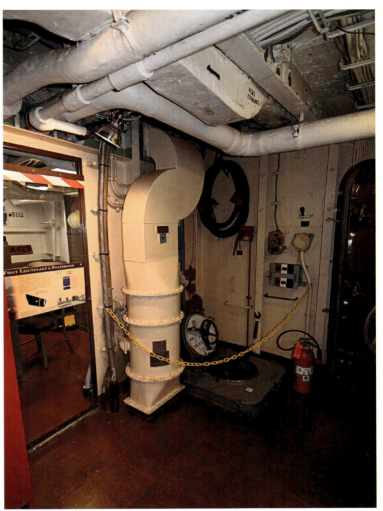

The entry to the first lieutenant's stateroom is viewed from another perspective. In addition to the aforementioned duties, the first lieutenant also was responsible for anchoring as well as maintenance of the ship's boats and the ship's hull and superstructure. *Rich Kolasa*

In the officers'-country passageway, the red locker to the right of center contains oxygen-breathing apparatus (OBA) equipment, for the use of damage-control personnel during fires. To the right is the entry to the first lieutenant's stateroom. The first lieutenant is a billet, not a rank, and his duties include commanding the deck department, which was responsible for such on-deck activities as mooring, seamanship, gunnery, and underway replenishment. *Rich Kolasa*

MUSEUM SHIP 133

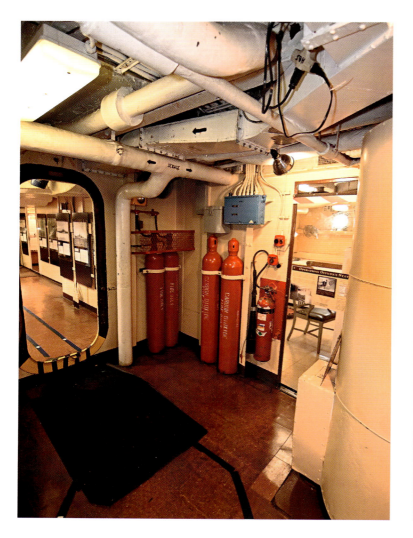

Stored in this corner of officers' country are four carbon dioxide bottles, for use in extinguishing fires. To the right is the stateroom of the operations officer, whose many responsibilities include the supervision of the ship's radar, communications, and combat information center. This officer also coordinates search-and-rescue missions, law-enforcement operations, and the gathering of intelligence. *Rich Kolasa*

An officer's stateroom includes a desk, chair, locker, cabinet with drawers, and single berth. Above the berth are a circulating fan, a lamp, and a porthole. *Rich Kolasa*

In this space are, *left*, a locker for repair equipment. To the right of the door at the center is a storage space for emergency cutting equipment, and a box for a spare oxyacetylene cutting rig. *Rich Kolasa*

The wardroom was the space for the officers to take their meals and relax. It included a mess area and a lounge. On the far side of the table is a binnacle, with an iron ball on each side, called a correction sphere, to counteract magnetic interference from the ship's hull. The binnacle is now used for collecting donations. Above the table is a surgical lamp, since in emergencies the wardroom would be used as a medical station. *Rich Kolasa*

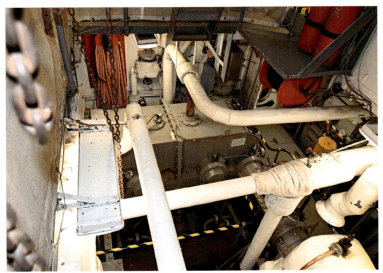

In the officers' pantry, cooks prepared meals for the cutter's officers. It is just forward of the officers' lounge and is equipped with an oven with a range and a grill on top, with a fryer to the side. *Rich Kolasa*

Part of the engine room is observed from above. Superheated steam from two boilers was routed to two Westinghouse double-reduction-geared turbines, each of which incorporated a high-pressure turbine and a low-pressure turbine. *Rich Kolasa*

MUSEUM SHIP

Turbines and steam ducts are packed into the engine room. From each turbine, a shaft transferred power to a reduction gear, from which a propeller shaft transmitted power to a propeller. *Rich Kolasa*

This passageway is in the amidships area. Toward the upper right is a curved frame with the stencil "FR 76," indicating that this is the seventy-sixth lateral frame of the ship. Frames are numbered consecutively, starting at 1, from the bow of the ship. The dark-blue appliances stored on the right are shores: portable, adjustable steel beams used by the damage-control personnel to buck up damaged areas of the hull until permanent repairs can be made. *Rich Kolasa*

This photo is of the same passageway in the preceding photo but was taken farther along in the passageway, looking in the opposite direction. At the center are a 220-volt portable, submersible pump and its power cable. In the event the hull was breached, this pump could be lowered into the infiltrating water to expel it. On the opposite side of the frame next to the pump is stored a section of 2½-inch hose, for use with the pump. *Rich Kolasa*

The engineering log office was in this compartment, amidships on the second deck. Here, the log books for the engineering department of the ship were stored and continually updated. *Rich Kolasa*

The crew's mess, where the enlisted men took their meals, is located amidships on the second deck. A serving counter and drink dispensers are in the background. *Rich Kolasa*

The enlisted men's berths are stacked three high and are equipped with ladders and handrails. To the left are several lockers, in which crewmen stored their clothing and personal items. *Rich Kolasa*

MUSEUM SHIP **137**

The enlisted men's berths are stacked three high and are equipped with ladders and handrails. To the left are several lockers, in which crewmen stored their clothing and personal items. *Rich Kolasa*

Several of the enlisted men's lockers contain displays of uniforms and crew memorabilia. *Rich Kolasa*

This corner of the enlisted men's quarters includes a locker for emergency cutting equipment (*right*) and a submersible pump and 2½-inch water hose, partially obscured by a gray duct (*left*). The door in the center background leads to the upper 5-inch/38-caliber-ammunition-handling room. The round, brass-colored object to the right of that door is a scuttle, a covered opening through which 5-inch/38-caliber ammunition would be passed from this compartment to the ammunition-handling room. *Rich Kolasa*

Just out of view to the left in the preceding photo is a 5-inch/38-caliber-ammunition hoist. This dredger-type hoist was used to bring up ammunition from magazines two decks below. From here the ammunition would be passed through the previously mentioned scuttle into the upper handling room. The tip of a 5-inch projectile is visible in the top of the hoist. *Rich Kolasa*

MUSEUM SHIP 139

The upper 5-inch/38-caliber-ammunition-handling room is visible through the door from the crew's quarters. From the upper handling room, ammunition, in the form of 5-inch projectiles and separate powder cartridges, was hoisted up into the 5-inch/38-caliber gun mount. *Rich Kolasa*

These 5-inch projectiles are stored in racks in the upper ammunition-handling room. The projectiles are painted blue to signify that they are inert training rounds. These projectiles weigh about 56 pounds each. *Rich Kolasa*

Two 5-inch/38-caliber dummy powder cartridges are displayed in the upper ammunition-handling room. The live cartridges weighed about 28 pounds. *Rich Kolasa*

The crew's head includes a row of lavatories and mirrors, seen here, as well as toilets and showers. A sign instructs the crew to "Turn water off when not in use," since fresh water was always a precious and scarce commodity on ships. *Rich Kolasa*

A Browning .50-caliber M2 HB machine gun is resting on a desk in the ship's armory, where small arms and ammunition and related equipment were securely stored. To the right is a mannequin wearing an orange wetsuit and a holstered pistol. The yellow sign to the left identifies this compartment as number A-105-A, located between frames 36 and 42. *Rich Kolasa*

To the forward port quarter of the pilothouse, on the navigating bridge, is an upholstered, swiveling seat with a footrest. Adjacent to it is a pelorus, an instrument used in navigation to maintain the bearing of the ship or establish the relative bearing of another ship or object. On the level above the pilothouse (*upper left*) are a whip antenna and a searchlight with a cover over it. *Rich Kolasa*

The interior of the pilothouse is viewed from the captain's chair on the starboard side. To the front of the chair are a radar console, the ship's steering wheel, and navigating instruments, including a gyrocompass repeater and a binnacle. In the left background is the engine-order telegraph. At the upper center is a speaking tube, for sending voice signals up to the flying bridge over the pilothouse. *Rich Kolasa*

In a view of the pilothouse from the port side, in the foreground is the engine-order telegraph. This was a signaling device, for transmitting directions for the speed and direction of the engines to the chief engineer in the engine room. On the near side is the handle for signaling directions for the port engine, with a dial marked with the various orders of the engine, including forward and reverse speeds and stop. On the opposite side of the telegraph is the handle for signaling the orders for the starboard engine. *Rich Kolasa*

MUSEUM SHIP 143

Specifications

Treasury-class cutter

Displacement	2,216 tons
Length	327 ft. overall
Beam	41 ft.
Draft	12.5 ft.

Propulsion

Boilers	2 oil-fueled Babcock & Wilcox
Fuel capacity	135,180 US gallons
Turbines	2 6,200 hp Westinghouse geared
Speed	20.5 knots
Range	12,300 nautical miles at 11 knots
Complement	1937: 12 officers, 4 warrants, 107 enlisted
	1941: 16 officers, 5 warrants, 200 enlisted
	1966: 10 officers, 3 warrants, 133 enlisted
	1986: 10 officers, 2 warrants, 117 enlisted

Detection

1945	Radar: SC, SG-1
	Fire control radar: Mk-26
	Sonar: QC series
1966	Radar: AN/SPS-29D; AN/SPA-52
	Fire control radar: Mk-26 MOD 4
	Sonar: AN/SQS-11

Armament

1936	3 × 5"/51 cal.
	2 × 6-pounders
	1 × 1-pounder
1941	2 × 5"/51 cal. guns
	4 × 3"/50 cal. guns
	2 × depth charge racks
	1 × "Y"-gun depth charge projector
1943	4 × 5"/38 cal. guns (only cutter in class to be so armed)
	8 × 20 mm/80 cal.
	1 × Hedgehog
	2 × depth charge racks
	6 × K-gun depth charge throwers
1945	2 × 5"/38 cal. turret
	6 × 40 mm/60 cal. (twin mount)
	4 × 20 mm/80 cal.
1946	1 × 5"/38 cal. turret
	1 × 40 mm/60 cal. (twin mount)
	2 × 20 mm/80 cal.
	1 × Hedgehog
	2 × depth charge racks
	? × depth charge projectors
1966	1 × 5"/38 cal. turret
	1 × Mk. 52 MOD3 director
	1 × Mk. 10-1 Hedgehog
	2 (P&S) × Mk. 32 MOD5TT
	4 × Mk. 44 MOD1 torpedoes
	2 × 50 cal. Mk. 2 Browning MG
	2 × Mk. 13 high-altitude parachute flare mortars
1986	1 × 5"/38 cal. turret
	2 × 50 cal. Mk. 2 Browning MG